Editors
Lorin Klistoff, M.A.
Marisa Maccarelli-Harris, M.A.

Managing Editor
Mara Ellen Guckian

Editor in Chief
Karen J. Goldfluss, M.S. Ed.

Cover Artist
Diem Pascarella

Art Coordinator
Renée Mc Elwee

Illustrator
Clint McKnight

Imaging
Leonard P. Swierski

Publisher

Mary D. Smith, M.S. Ed.

TCR 2553

Instant Math Practice

Grade 3

Standards-based exercises for year-round practice!

- *Number and Operations*
- *Algebra*
- *Geometry*
- *Measurement and Data*
- *Problem Solving*

w x h

Teacher Created Resources

Author

Damon James

Teacher Created Resources
6421 Industry Way
Westminster, C
www.teachercre
ISBN: 978-1-420
© 2013 Teacher Creat
Made in U.S.A.

D1305860

Teacher Created Resources

Table of Contents

Introduction

The *Instant Math Practice* series was written to provide students with frequent opportunities to master and retain important math skills. The unit practice pages are designed to target and reinforce those skills. As students become active learners and discover important mathematical relationships, they are more likely to improve their problem-solving skills and gain confidence in math. When using this book, take every opportunity possible to incorporate the practice exercises into your current curriculum.

This book addresses a variety of math skills and topics that help students build foundational knowledge in the following areas: numbers and numeration, addition, subtraction, multiplication, division, fractions, decimals, money, two- and three-dimensional objects, length, capacity, problem solving, and so much more. In addition, the multiple-practice opportunities in each unit facilitate students' mastery of math skills and concepts.

How to Use the Activity Pages

There are over 120 student activity pages, with each page containing six practice sections. The contents of each practice page relate directly to the skill named on that page. However, each of the six sections is designed to allow students to practice the skill in different ways. For example, on a page that focuses on place value, students may be asked to represent an expanded number as a numeral, to write a numeral in a chart to show its place value, to express the value of a digit in the given numeral, or to show a number in word form. By offering a variety of ways to practice a math skill on any given page, students think about and learn multiple approaches to mastering that skill.

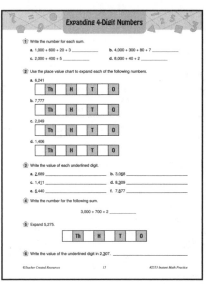

There are several ways in which to use the activities in this book. You may wish to coordinate each unit with whatever math concept is being introduced to the class. The student pages can be used to pre- or post-assess students as well. Practice pages can be assigned as homework or additional class work. An answer key is included in the back of the book.

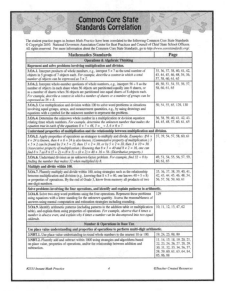

Common Core State Standards Correlations (CCSS)

Correlations have been provided for Common Core State Standards for Math. For quick viewing of the math correlations, a chart is provided on pages 4 and 5 of this book. (*Note*: This version does not contain page titles but does reference the page numbers.) For a printable PDF version of the correlations chart, go to *www.teachercreated.com/standards/*. These charts correlate student page activities to applicable standards within a given domain.

Common Core State Standards Correlation

The student practice pages in *Instant Math Practice* have been correlated to the following Common Core State Standards © Copyright 2010. National Governors Association Center for Best Practices and Council of Chief State School Officers. All rights reserved. For more information about the Common Core State Standards, go to *http://www.corestandards.org/*.

Mathematics Standards	Page
Operations & Algebraic Thinking	
Represent and solve problems involving multiplication and division.	
3.OA.1. Interpret products of whole numbers, e.g., interpret 5 × 7 as the total number of objects in 5 groups of 7 objects each. *For example, describe a context in which a total number of objects can be expressed as 5 × 7.*	35, 36, 37, 38, 40, 41, 42, 43, 44, 45, 46, 48, 54, 56, 57, 58, 60, 61, 65
3.OA.2. Interpret whole-number quotients of whole numbers, e.g., interpret 56 ÷ 8 as the number of objects in each share when 56 objects are partitioned equally into 8 shares, or as a number of shares when 56 objects are partitioned into equal shares of 8 objects each. *For example, describe a context in which a number of shares or a number of groups can be expressed as 56 ÷ 8.*	49, 50, 51, 54, 55, 56, 57, 58, 60, 61, 65
3.OA.3. Use multiplication and division within 100 to solve word problems in situations involving equal groups, arrays, and measurement quantities, e.g., by using drawings and equations with a symbol for the unknown number to represent the problem.	50, 54, 55, 65, 129, 130
3.OA.4. Determine the unknown whole number in a multiplication or division equation relating three whole numbers. *For example, determine the unknown number that makes the equation true in each of the equations 8 × ? = 48, 5 = _ ÷ 3, 6 × 6 = ?*	36, 38, 39, 40, 41, 42, 43, 44, 45, 48, 57, 60, 61, 65
Understand properties of multiplication and the relationship between multiplication and division.	
3.OA.5. Apply properties of operations as strategies to multiply and divide. *Examples: If 6 × 4 = 24 is known, then 4 × 6 = 24 is also known. (Commutative property of multiplication.) 3 × 5 × 2 can be found by 3 × 5 = 15, then 15 × 2 = 30, or by 5 × 2 = 10, then 3 × 10 = 30. (Associative property of multiplication.) Knowing that 8 × 5 = 40 and 8 × 2 = 16, one can find 8 × 7 as 8 × (5 + 2) = (8 × 5) + (8 × 2) = 40 + 16 = 56. (Distributive property.)*	37, 39, 54, 57, 58, 60, 61
3.OA.6. Understand division as an unknown-factor problem. *For example, find 32 ÷ 8 by finding the number that makes 32 when multiplied by 8.*	49, 51, 54, 55, 56, 57, 59, 60, 61, 65
Multiply and divide within 100.	
3.OA.7. Fluently multiply and divide within 100, using strategies such as the relationship between multiplication and division (e.g., knowing that 8 × 5 = 40, one knows 40 ÷ 5 = 8) or properties of operations. By the end of Grade 3, know from memory all products of two one-digit numbers.	35, 36, 37, 38, 39, 40, 41, 42, 43, 44, 45, 46, 48, 54, 56, 57, 58, 59, 60, 61
Solve problems involving the four operations, and identify and explain patterns in arithmetic.	
3.OA.8. Solve two-step word problems using the four operations. Represent these problems using equations with a letter standing for the unknown quantity. Assess the reasonableness of answers using mental computation and estimation strategies including rounding.	129
3.OA.9. Identify arithmetic patterns (including patterns in the addition table or multiplication table), and explain them using properties of operations. *For example, observe that 4 times a number is always even, and explain why 4 times a number can be decomposed into two equal addends.*	10, 11, 12, 13, 47, 62
Number & Operations in Base Ten	
Use place value understanding and properties of operations to perform multi-digit arithmetic.	
3.NBT.1. Use place value understanding to round whole numbers to the nearest 10 or 100.	19, 24, 25, 88, 89
3.NBT.2. Fluently add and subtract within 1000 using strategies and algorithms based on place value, properties of operations, and/or the relationship between addition and subtraction.	11, 14, 15, 18, 19, 20, 21, 22, 23, 24, 26, 27, 28, 29, 30, 31, 32, 33, 34, 56, 57, 58, 59, 60, 61, 63, 64, 84, 85, 86, 88

Common Core State Standards Correlation

Number & Operations in Base Ten (cont.)	
3.NBT.3. Multiply one-digit whole numbers by multiples of 10 in the range 10–90 (e.g., 9 × 80, 5 × 60) using strategies based on place value and properties of operations.	10, 38, 39, 40, 42, 43, 44, 45, 54, 61

Number & Operations - Fractions	
Develop understanding of fractions as numbers.	
3.NF.1. Understand a fraction 1/*b* as the quantity formed by 1 part when *a* whole is partitioned into *b* equal parts; understand a fraction *a*/*b* as the quantity formed by a parts of size 1/*b*.	66, 67, 68, 69, 70, 71, 72, 76, 77, 78, 82
3.NF.2. Understand a fraction as a number on the number line; represent fractions on a number line diagram.	68, 74, 77, 78, 82
3.NF.3. Explain equivalence of fractions in special cases, and compare fractions by reasoning about their size.	68, 70, 71, 72, 73, 78

Measurement & Data	
Solve problems involving measurement and estimation.	
3.MD.1. Tell and write time to the nearest minute and measure time intervals in minutes. Solve word problems involving addition and subtraction of time intervals in minutes, e.g., by representing the problem on a number line diagram.	110, 111, 112
3.MD.2. Measure and estimate liquid volumes and masses of objects using standard units of grams (g), kilograms (kg), and liters (l). Add, subtract, multiply, or divide to solve one-step word problems involving masses or volumes that are given in the same units, e.g., by using drawings (such as a beaker with a measurement scale) to represent the problem.	120, 121, 122, 123
Represent and interpret data.	
3.MD.3. Draw a scaled picture graph and a scaled bar graph to represent a data set with several categories. Solve one- and two-step "how many more" and "how many less" problems using information presented in scaled bar graphs. *For example, draw a bar graph in which each square in the bar graph might represent 5 pets.*	126, 127, 128
3.MD.4. Generate measurement data by measuring lengths using rulers marked with halves and fourths of an inch. Show the data by making a line plot, where the horizontal scale is marked off in appropriate units—whole numbers, halves, or quarters.	113, 115, 118
Geometric measurement: understand concepts of area and relate area to multiplication and to addition.	
3.MD.5. Recognize area as an attribute of plane figures and understand concepts of area measurement.	119
3.MD.6. Measure areas by counting unit squares (square cm, square m, square in, square ft, and improvised units).	119
3.MD.7. Relate area to the operations of multiplication and addition.	119
Geometric measurement: recognize perimeter.	
3.MD.8. Solve real world and mathematical problems involving perimeters of polygons, including finding the perimeter given the side lengths, finding an unknown side length, and exhibiting rectangles with the same perimeter and different areas or with the same area and different perimeters.	118

Geometry	
Reason with shapes and their attributes.	
3.G.1. Understand that shapes in different categories (e.g., rhombuses, rectangles, and others) may share attributes (e.g., having four sides), and that the shared attributes can define a larger category (e.g., quadrilaterals). Recognize rhombuses, rectangles, and squares as examples of quadrilaterals, and draw examples of quadrilaterals that do not belong to any of these subcategories.	91, 92, 93, 94, 95

Numbers to 999

1 Write the number shown by the base ten blocks.

a.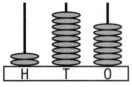

_____

b.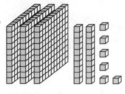

_____

c.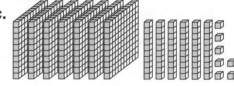

_____

2 Write the number shown by the abacus.

a.

| H | T | O |

_____

b.

| H | T | O |

_____

c.

| H | T | O |

_____

3 Write each of the following numbers in words.

a. 226 _____

b. 56 _____

c. 102 _____

4 Write each number as a numeral.

a. one hundred sixty-two _____   **b.** nine hundred two _____

5 Write the number shown by the base ten blocks.   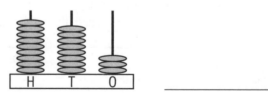 _____

6 Write the number shown by the abacus.   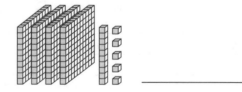 _____

7 Write *621* in words. _____

8 Write *three hundred sixteen* as a numeral. _____

1 Write the number shown by the base ten blocks or the abacus.

a.

b.

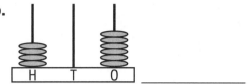

2 What is the value of the 5 in each of the following numbers?

a. 215 _____   **b.** 506 _____   **c.** 352 _____

3 Circle the greater number.

a. 206 or 306   **b.** 111 or 101   **c.** 227 or 272

4 Write the number shown.

a.

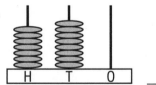

b.

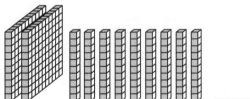

5 What is the value of the 5 in the number 650? _____

6 Circle the greater number.   215 or 251

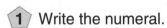
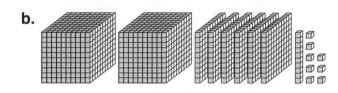

1 Write the numeral.

a.

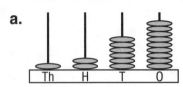

Th H T O

_____

b.

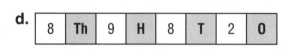

_____

c. | 9 | **Th** | 3 | **H** | 4 | **T** | 6 | **O** |

_____

d. | 8 | **Th** | 9 | **H** | 8 | **T** | 2 | **O** |

_____

2 Write as a numeral.

a. two thousand six hundred eighty _____

b. six thousand seven hundred six _____

3 Write in words.

a. 6,308 _____

_____

b. 5,251 _____

_____

c. 1,006 _____

_____

4 Write the numeral.

a. | 5 | **Th** | 0 | **H** | 2 | **T** | 1 | **O** |

_____

b.

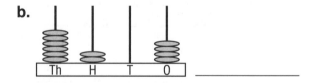

Th H T O _____

5 Write *three thousand forty-nine* as a numeral. _____

6 Write *2,346* in words. _____

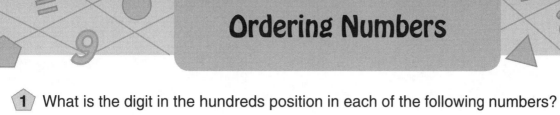

Ordering Numbers

1 What is the digit in the hundreds position in each of the following numbers?

    a. 206 _____   **b.** 2,168 _____   **c.** 39 _____

2 True or false?

    a. 426 > 416 _____   **b.** 871 < 325 _____   **c.** 872 < 596 _____

    d. 285 > 125 _____   **e.** 1,089 > 1,000 _____   **f.** 2,467 < 2,264 _____

3 Order the following numbers from *least* to *greatest*.

    a. 220, 210, 236, 206 _____

    b. 786, 687, 678, 876 _____

4 Order the numbers from *greatest* to *least*.

    a. 301, 205, 603, 103 _____

    b. 119, 125, 108, 132 _____

5 What is the digit in the hundreds position in the number 15,082? _____

6 True or false?

    a. 989 < 998 _____

    b. 604 > 640 _____

    c. 1,720 < 1,728 _____

7 Order the numbers from *least* to *greatest*.

    208, 691, 298, 198 _____

8 Order the numbers from *greatest* to *least*.

    526, 896, 325, 696 _____

Counting by Tens

1 Count the total number of pencils.

a.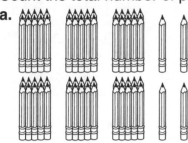

_____

b.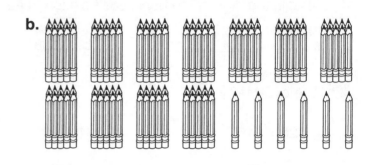

_____

c.

_____

d.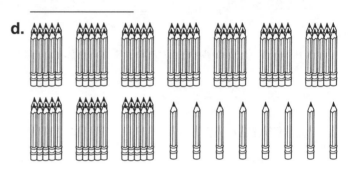

_____

2 Count forward by tens to complete the sequence.

a. 10, 20, 30, _____, _____, _____

b. 100, 110, 120, _____, _____, _____

c. 82, 92, _____, 112, _____

d. 403, 413, _____, _____, 443

3 Count backward by tens to complete the sequence.

a. 100, 90, 80, _____, _____, _____

b. 500, 490, 480, _____, _____, _____

c. 77, 67, 57, _____, _____, _____

d. 295, _____, 275, 265, _____

4 Count the total number of pencils.

_____

5 Count forward by tens to complete the sequence.

56, 66, 76, _____, _____, _____

6 Count backward by tens to complete the sequence.

122, 112, 102, _____, _____, _____

Counting by Hundreds

1 Complete the table.

	100 Less	Number	100 More
a.		400	
b.		550	
c.		921	
d.		763	
e.		1,230	
f.		1,569	

2 Count forward by hundreds to complete the sequences.

a. 100, 200, 300, _____, _____, _____ **b.** 98, 198, 298, _____, _____, _____

c. 451, 551, 651, _____, _____, _____ **d.** 750, 850, 950, _____, _____, _____

3 Count backward by hundreds to complete the sequences.

a. 900, 800, 700, _____, _____, _____ **b.** 801, 701, 601, _____, _____, _____

c. 560, 460, 360, _____, _____, _____ **d.** 799, 699, 599, _____, _____, _____

4 Complete the chart.

	100 Less	Number	100 More
a.		865	
b.		199	

5 Count forward by hundreds to complete the sequence.

1,485; 1,585; 1,685; _____; _____

6 Count backward by hundreds to complete the sequence.

763, 663, 563, _____, _____, _____

1

Start at . . .

a. 25 and count forward 3. ___28___   **b.** 25 and count forward 8. _____

c. 25 and count forward 9. _____   **d.** 25 and count forward 11. _____

e. 25 and count forward 6. _____   **f.** 25 and count forward 5. _____

2

Start at . . .

a. 39 and count backward 5. _____   **b.** 39 and count backward 9. _____

c. 39 and count backward 7. _____   **d.** 39 and count backward 11. _____

e. 39 and count backward 3. _____   **f.** 39 and count backward 20. _____

3

Start at 51.

a. Go forward 6. _____   **b.** Then go forward 5. _____

c. Then go backward 3. _____   **d.** Then go backward 2. _____

e. Then go forward 7. _____   **f.** Then go backward 10. _____

4

Start at 36 and count forward 6. _____

5 Start at 23 and count backward 5. _____

6 Start at 32 and go forward 6 and then backward 8. _____

Patterns

1 Continue the pattern modeled with the shapes.

a. ▲ ■ ▲ ■   _____ _____ _____

b. ▲ ▼ ▲ ▼   _____ _____ _____

c.    _____ _____ _____

d.   _____ _____ _____

2 Complete each number pattern.

a. 2, 4, 6, _____, _____, _____   **b.** 8, 16, 24, _____, _____, _____

c. 1, 3, 5, _____, _____, _____   **d.** 10, 15, 20, _____, _____, _____

e. 6, 9, 12, _____, _____, _____   **f.** 21, 23, 25, _____, _____, _____

3 Use words to describe each pattern.

a. 4, 8, 12, 16 _____

b. 48, 24, 12, 6 _____

c. 1, 2, 4, 8, 16 _____

4 Continue the pattern.

_____ _____ _____

5 Complete the following pattern: 10, 14, 18, _____, _____, _____.

6 Use words to describe the following pattern: 7, 10, 13, 16, 19.

_____

Expanding 3-Digit Numbers

1 Use the place value chart to expand the numbers.

a. 226

	H		T		O

b. 409

	H		T		O

c. 670

	H		T		O

d. 111

	H		T		O

e. 80

	H		T		O

f. 802

	H		T		O

2 Write the number for each of the following sums.

a. 600 + 20 + 5 _____

b. 200 + 60 + 9 _____

c. 300 + 7 _____

d. 800 + 30 + 6 _____

e. 400 + 80 _____

f. 900 + 90 + 9 _____

3 Write the value of each underlined digit.

a. 646 _____

b. 293 _____

c. 411 _____

d. 853 _____

e. 198 _____

f. 260 _____

4 Expand the number 507.

	H		T		O

5 Write the number for 700 + 3. _____

6 Write the value of the underlined digit. 315 _____

1 Write the number for each sum.

a. 1,000 + 600 + 20 + 3 _____   **b.** 4,000 + 300 + 80 + 7 _____

c. 2,000 + 400 + 5 _____   **d.** 8,000 + 40 + 2 _____

2 Use the place value chart to expand each of the following numbers.

a. 6,241

	Th		H		T		O

b. 7,777

	Th		H		T		O

c. 2,049

	Th		H		T		O

d. 1,406

	Th		H		T		O

3 Write the value of each underlined digit.

a. <u>2</u>,689 _____   **b.** 3,0<u>6</u>8 _____

c. 1,4<u>1</u>1 _____   **d.** 8,<u>3</u>09 _____

e. <u>6</u>,440 _____   **f.** 7,<u>8</u>77 _____

4 Write the number for the following sum.

3,000 + 700 + 2 _____

5 Expand 5,275.

	Th		H		T		O

6 Write the value of the underlined digit in 2,3<u>0</u>7. _____

4-Digit Numbers

1 Use the place value chart to expand each of the numbers.

a. 4,526

	Th		H		T		O

b. 6,049

	Th		H		T		O

c. 8,407

	Th		H		T		O

d. 9,260

	Th		H		T		O

2 Write each set of numbers from *least* to *greatest*.

a. 8,752; 7,582; 8,572; 2,578

_____

b. 1,999; 3,420; 2,870; 2,500

_____

c. 870; 249; 1,672; 972

_____

d. 1,111; 4,213; 2,671; 1,098

_____

3 Write the greatest number possible using all the digits supplied.

a. 1, 4, 9, 2 _____   **b.** 3, 6, 7, 8 _____

c. 3, 2, 4, 8 _____   **d.** 2, 6, 6, 4 _____

e. 1, 0, 9, 2 _____   **f.** 1, 2, 4, 3 _____

4 Expand the number 2,310.

	Th		H		T		O

5 Write the set of numbers from *least* to *greatest*.

1,021; 1,051; 1,161; 909; 1,211

_____

6 Write the greatest number possible using all the digits.

1, 8, 9, 3 _____

Less Than and Greater Than

1

A	B	C	D
ants	butterflies	caterpillars	dragonflies

Look at the groups of insects and use the correct inequality sign, < or >, to make each statement true.

a. A ☐ B

b. B ☐ C

c. C ☐ D

d. C ☐ A

e. B ☐ D

f. A ☐ D

2 Write *true* or *false* for each number sentence.

a. 340 < 350 _____

b. 925 < 920 _____

c. 102 < 109 _____

d. 425 > 396 _____

e. 756 > 790 _____

f. 210 > 220 _____

3 Use the correct inequality sign, < or >, to make each statement true.

a. 72 ☐ 76

b. 115 ☐ 126

c. 212 ☐ 200

d. 3,261 ☐ 3,200

e. 4,209 ☐ 4,290

f. 2,560 ☐ 2,650

4 Look at the groups of shapes in the box. Use the correct inequality sign, < or >, to make the statement true.

A ☐ B

5 Write *true* or *false* for 226 < 230. _____

6 Use the correct inequality sign, < or >, to make the statement true.

2,469 ☐ 2,508

Looking for Ten
When Adding

1 Look for sums of 10 first when adding the numbers. The first one is done for you.

   a.   3 →   3
       4 ⟩ =10
       + 6
         13

   b.   7
        3
       + 5

   c.   9
        6
       + 1

   d.   8
        2
       + 2

   e.   5
        6
       + 5

   f.   1
        3
       + 9

2 Look for sums of 10 or 20 first when adding the numbers below.

   a. 4 + 3 + 16 = _____

   b. 5 + 7 + 5 = _____

   c. 12 + 2 + 8 = _____

   d. 13 + 7 + 9 = _____

   e. 18 + 3 + 2 = _____

   f. 4 + 8 + 6 = _____

3 **a.** There are 3 pencils, 6 pens, and 7 crayons on the table. How many items are there all together? _____

   b. There are 6 trucks, 4 cars, and 7 motorcycles in the parking lot. How many vehicles are there all together? _____

   c. There are 5 apples, 2 pears, and 5 oranges on the table. How many pieces of fruit are there all together? _____

4 Look for sums of 10 first when adding.

       8
       2
     + 9

5 Look for sums of 10 or 20 first when adding.

       15 + 6 + 5 = _____

6 There are 3 toy sheep, 8 toy horses, and 7 toy cars on the floor. How many toys are there all together? _____

Adding with Regrouping to 99

1 Estimate each sum first by rounding each number to the nearest ten. Then solve each problem.

	Estimate	Actual		Estimate	Actual
a. 18 + 15	_____	_____	**b.** 28 + 35	_____	_____
c. 52 + 39	_____	_____	**d.** 17 + 37	_____	_____

2 Complete the problems by filling in the blanks.

a. 38 + 19 = 38 + 10 + 9 = _____

b. 45 + 28 = 45 + 20 + 8 = _____

c. 27 + 36 = 27 + 30 + _____ = _____

d. 48 + 15 = 48 + 10 + _____ = _____

3 Add.

a.
T	O
7	7
+	9

b.
T	O
4	5
+	8

c.
T	O
6	6
+	5

d.
T	O
6	5
+ 2	8

e.
T	O
3	7
+ 2	7

f.
T	O
3	6
+ 5	7

4 Estimate the sum first by rounding each number to the nearest ten. Then solve.

	Estimate	Actual
76 + 17	_____	_____

5 Complete the problem by filling in the blanks. 56 + 37 = 56 + _____ + _____ = _____

6 Add.
T	O
4	3
+ 2	9

1 Find each sum.

a.
T	O
3	9
2	4
+ 1	3

b.
T	O
1	6
2	8
+ 3	9

c.
T	O
3	0
3	4
+ 1	7

d.
T	O
1	4
3	6
+ 2	3

2 Find the totals.

a. 27 eggs, 25 eggs, and 29 eggs _____

b. 15 fish, 23 fish, and 19 fish _____

c. 22 candies, 19 candies, and 30 candies _____

3 Complete each magic square. The numbers in each row (up, down, across, diagonally) should have a sum equal to the number given above the square.

a. (15)
4	9	2
8		6

b. (33)
14	9	10
12		8

c. (36)
11		
	12	
15		13

d. (21)
	7	
10	3	8

4 Find the sum.
T	O
1	7
1	6
+ 2	5

5 What is the total cost of $22, $14, and $28? _____

6 Complete the magic square. 66

28	18	20
		16

Adding 3-Digit Numbers with Regrouping

1 Add. Regroup when needed.

a.

H	T	O
7	0	8
+ 2	0	6

b.

H	T	O
4	3	6
+ 4	3	6

c.

H	T	O
6	2	8
+ 3	0	4

d.

H	T	O
7	3	9
+ 2	4	6

2 Add.

a.
$$372$$
$$+259$$

b.
$$688$$
$$+185$$

c.
$$173$$
$$+258$$

d.
$$238$$
$$+398$$

3

$155	$180	$376	$567	$298	$265
Game Controller	**TV**	**Bed**	**Couch**	**DVD Player**	**Desk**

a. How much will a TV and a DVD player cost? _____

b. How much will a game controller and a desk cost? _____

c. How much will a couch and a bed cost? _____

d. How much will a bed and a DVD player cost? _____

4 Add.

H	T	O
4	5	6
+ 1	2	8

5 Add.
$$4 \quad 3 \quad 8$$
$$+ 2 \quad 9 \quad 6$$

6 Use the price list above to find the cost of a TV and a desk. Show your work in the box.

Mental Math

1 Mental Math: Add.

    a. 200 + 700 = _____   **b.** 800 + 300 = _____

    c. 900 + 800 = _____   **d.** 600 + 500 = _____

    e. 700 + 700 = _____   **f.** 500 + 900 = _____

2 Find the answers by making multiples of ten first. The first one has been done for you.

    a. 37 + 6 = 37 + 3 + 3   **b.** 28 + 8 = 28 + ____ + ____

           =   40 + 3   =   30 + ____

           = 43   = _____

    c. 42 + 9 = 42 + ____ + ____   **d.** 38 + 5 = 38 + ____ + ____

           = ____ + ____   = ____ + ____

           = ____   = ____

    e. 29 + 7 = 29 + ____ + ____   **f.** 64 + 7 = 64 + ____ + ____

           = ____ + ____   = ____ + ____

           = ____   = ____

3 Find the following sums by looking for multiples of ten first.

    a. 7 + 3 + 4 = _____   **b.** 12 + 6 + 8 = _____

    c. 4 + 3 + 16 = _____   **d.** 19 + 8 + 1 = _____

    e. 5 + 7 + 15 = _____   **f.** 7 + 6 + 13 = _____

4 Mental Math: Add. 600 + 300 = _____

5 Find the sum by looking for a multiple of ten. 11 + 8 + 9 = _____

6 Add mentally by making a multiple of ten first. 26 + 9 = _____

1 A doll costs $8, a ball costs $4, a teddy bear costs $7, and a hat costs $3. If a hat, a teddy bear, and a ball are purchased, what is the total cost?

_____

Show your work for question 1.

2 Add. $3 + 4 + 7 + 5 =$ _____

3 Find the missing number. $21 +$ _____ $= 35$

4 Selecting from the following numbers, write two different sums that equal 48.

24   34   14   40   18   30   32

_____ + _____ = 48

_____ + _____ = 48

5 There are 14 boys, 13 girls, and a teacher in the class. How many people are in the classroom? _____

6 Fill-in the boxes.

$$
\begin{array}{r}
2\ \square \\
+\ \square\ 6 \\
\hline
7\ 9
\end{array}
$$

7 Thirty-five sheep and twenty-seven cows were in the pasture. How many animals were there all together? _____

8 Create four different addition problems with sums of 52.

_____ + _____ = 52   _____ + _____ = 52

$$
\begin{array}{r}
+\ \underline{\quad\quad} \\
5\ 2
\end{array}
\qquad
\begin{array}{r}
+\ \underline{\quad\quad} \\
5\ 2
\end{array}
$$

9 You have $100 to spend, and you must spend all your money. What could you buy from the items below? Find at least two different combinations.

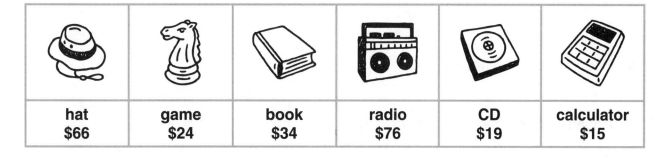

| hat $66 | game $24 | book $34 | radio $76 | CD $19 | calculator $15 |

Combination 1: _____

Combination 2: _____

Rounding Numbers

1 Round each number to the nearest hundred.

    a. 215 _____

    b. 329 _____

    c. 476 _____

    d. 190 _____

    e. 520 _____

    f. 388 _____

2 Round each number to the nearest ten.

    a. 172 _____

    b. 429 _____

    c. 863 _____

    d. 411 _____

    e. 397 _____

    f. 208 _____

3 Round each number to the nearest ten to estimate the solution.

    a.   31 + 63
     ≈ 30 + 60 ____ ____
     ≈   90 ____

    b.   39 + 41
     ≈ ____ + ____
     ≈ ____

    c.   81 + 22
     ≈ ____ + ____
     ≈ ____

    d.   59 − 22
     ≈ ____ − ____
     ≈ ____

    e.   87 − 31
     ≈ ____ − ____
     ≈ ____

    f.   71 − 28
     ≈ ____ − ____
     ≈ ____

4 Round 482 to the nearest hundred. _____

5 Round 822 to the nearest ten. _____

6 Round each number to the nearest 10 to estimate each solution.

    a. 69 + 23 = _____

    b. 97 − 48 = _____

Estimating

1 Round each number to the nearest ten, and then circle the best estimate.

   a.   9   +   6   +   15   +   20

      Estimate: ____ + ____ + ____ + ____   ≈   20   or   60   or   100

   b.   15   +   20   +   25   +   30

      Estimate: ____ + ____ + ____ + ____   ≈   10   or   50   or   100

2 Round each number to the nearest ten, and then circle the best estimate.

   a.   30   +   60   +   50   +   21

      Estimate: ____ + ____ + ____ + ____   ≈   130   or   160   or   190

   b.   46   +   24   +   59   +   63

      Estimate: ____ + ____ + ____ + ____   ≈   150   or   190   or   230

3 Round each number to the nearest ten, and then circle the best estimate.

   a.   90   –   1   –   1   –   1   –   1

      Estimate: ____ – ____ – ____ – ____ – ____   ≈   90   or   70   or   50

   b.   140   –   8   –   6   –   5   –   2   –   7

      Estimate: ____ – ____ – ____ – ____ – ____ – ____   ≈   120   or   90   or   100

4 Circle the best estimate (use nearest ten).

    8 + 5 + 7 + 21 ≈   20   or   50   or   70

5 Circle the best estimate (use nearest ten).

    19 + 76 + 25 + 37 ≈   90   or   130   or   170

6 Circle the best estimate (use nearest ten).

    130 – 7 – 7 – 7 – 7 ≈   120   or   90   or   60

Subtraction

1 Find each result.

a. 10 take away 6 = _____

b. 17 minus 5 = _____

c. the difference between 12 and 2 = _____

d. subtract 8 from 10 = _____

e. 14 take away 3 = _____

f. 9 minus 7 = _____

2 Use the number line to help find the differences.

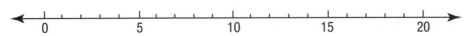

a. $14 - 9 =$ _____

b. $12 - 4 =$ _____

c. $18 - 12 =$ _____

d. $19 - 7 =$ _____

e. $16 - 7 =$ _____

f. $15 - 11 =$ _____

3 Write a number sentence for each set of pictures.

a.

b.

c.

_____

_____

_____

d.

e.

f.

_____

_____

_____

4 Subtract 4 from 14. _____

5 Find the difference. $13 - 7 =$ _____ (Use the number line in question 2 to help.)

6 Write a number sentence.

 _____

Subtraction Patterns

1 Complete the following problems.

a. 9 – 4 = _____

    90 – 40 = _____

    900 – 400 = _____

b. 8 – 1 = _____

    80 – 10 = _____

    800 – 100 = _____

c. 8 – 4 = _____

    80 – 40 = _____

    800 – 400 = _____

d. 7 – 5 = _____

    70 – 50 = _____

    700 – 500 = _____

2 Write a number sentence and solve.

a.

b.

c.

_____   _____   _____

3 Complete.

a. 8 + 3 = 11   11 – _____ = 8   11 – _____ = 3

b. 12 + 8 = 20   20 – _____ = 8   20 – _____ = 12

c. 14 + 5 = 19   19 – _____ = 5   19 – _____ = 14

d. 9 + 6 = 15   15 – _____ = 6   15 – _____ = 9

4 Complete.   10 – 3 = _____   100 – 30 = _____   1,000 – 300 = _____

5 Subtract.    _____

6 Complete.   8 + 7 = 15   15 – _____ = 7   15 – _____ = 8

1 Use the given strategy to solve the problems. The first one has been done for you.

a. 30 – 12: **think**   30 – 10 – 2

= ___20___ – 2

= ___18___

b. 24 – 11: **think**   24 – 10 – 1

= _____ – 1

= _____

c. 46 – 13: **think**   46 – _____ – 3

= _____ – 3

= _____

d. 47 – 22: **think**   47 – _____ – _____

= _____ – _____

= _____

e. 30 – 12: **think**   39 – _____ – _____

= _____ – _____

= _____

f. 36 – 23: **think**   36 – _____ – _____

= _____ – _____

= _____

2 Solve the problems using the strategy given in question number 1 above.

a. 45 – 13 = _____

b. 50 – 16 = _____

c. 29 – 17 = _____

d. 38 – 23 = _____

3 Solve.

a.

T	O
2	7
– 1	2

b.

T	O
4	9
–	7

c.

T	O
1	9
–	8

d.

T	O
3	6
– 1	4

4 Use the strategy from question number 1 to solve the problem.

49 – 28: **think** 49 – _____ – _____ = _____

5 Find the answer. 49 – 17 = _____

6 Solve.

T	O
5	6
– 1	4

1 Complete.

a.
T	O
9	6
− 1	5

b.
T	O
7	7
− 3	5

c.
T	O
6	3
− 4	1

d.
T	O
8	9
− 4	7

2 Complete.

a.
T	O
5	9
− 2	☐
3	3

b.
T	O
9	9
− ☐	8
2	1

c.
T	O
6	6
− 4	☐
2	4

d.
T	O
8	5
− ☐	1
1	4

3 Solve. Show your work in the box.

a. 55 birds; 24 flew away
How many are left?

b. 79 candles; 38 used
How many remain?

_____

_____

c. 39 girls and 14 boys
How many *more* girls than boys?

d. 46 cats and 21 dogs
How many *more* cats than dogs?

_____

_____

4 Subtract.
T	O
8	4
− 2	3

5 Complete.
T	O
7	7
− ☐	☐
2	5

6 Solve. 49 apples; 23 picked. How many are left? _____

1 Subtract.

a.	T	O
	2	4
−		8

b.	T	O
	4	2
−		9

c.	T	O
	7	1
−		8

d.	T	O
	5	3
−		9

2 Subtract.

a.	T	O
	7	4
−	1	6

b.	T	O
	6	5
−	3	7

c.	T	O
	9	1
−	7	6

d.	T	O
	8	3
−	2	5

3 Subtract. Check your subtraction by adding.

a.
	5	3	→	☐	☐
−	2	5	+	2	5
				5	3

b.
	8	3	→	☐	☐
−	4	6	+	4	6
				8	3

c.
	9	2	→	☐	☐
−	7	5	+	7	5
				☐	☐

d.
	7	5	→	☐	☐
−	2	9	+	2	9
				☐	☐

4 Subtract.

	T	O
	5	2
−		8

5 Subtract.

	T	O
	5	3
−	2	6

6 Subtract. Check your subtraction by adding.

	9	1	→	☐	☐
−	6	4	+	6	4
				☐	☐

1 Find the missing digits in the subtraction problems.

a.
```
    9  3  5
 - [ ] 2 [ ]
 -----------
    2  1  3
```

b.
```
    4  9  9
 -  3  4 [ ]
 -----------
   [ ] 5  6
```

c.
```
    7  5  6
 - [ ][ ] 5
 -----------
    2  1 [ ]
```

d.
```
   [ ][ ] 6
 -  6  4 [ ]
 -----------
    2  5  3
```

2 The following children have been saving for a television. Find how much more each person needs to save before he or she has enough money for the television.

$529

a. Steve has saved $345. _____

b. Anton has saved $517. _____

c. Coral has saved $479. _____

d. Anita has saved $395. _____

3

A12	B69	D50	G16	P80
$290	$169	$427	$399	$345

What change would I get from . . .

a. $250 if I bought the B69? _____

b. $350 if I bought the A12? _____

c. $500 if I bought the D50? _____

4 Find the missing digits.

```
    3 [ ] 8
 -  2  4 [ ]
 -----------
   [ ] 5  6
```

5 How much more does Morgan need to save if she has $375 towards the $529 television?

_____

6 For the printers in question 3, what is the difference in price between P80 and B69?

_____

Subtraction Strategies

1 Use the chart to find each number by counting backward.

1	2	3	4	5	6	7	8	9	10
11	12	13	14	15	16	17	18	19	20
21	22	23	24	25	26	27	28	29	30
31	32	33	34	35	36	37	38	39	40
41	42	43	44	45	46	47	48	49	50
51	52	53	54	55	56	57	58	59	60
61	62	63	64	65	66	67	68	69	70
71	72	73	74	75	76	77	78	79	80
81	82	83	84	85	86	87	88	89	90
91	92	93	94	95	96	97	98	99	100

a. 8 less than 20 _____

b. 5 less than 12 _____

c. 7 less than 34 _____

d. 8 less than 74 _____

e. 9 less than 84 _____

f. 6 less than 91 _____

2 Find the answers by counting backward. Use the chart above if needed.

a. Damon needs 65 cents. He has 50 cents. How much more does he need? _____

b. 43 pins were lost. Kobi found 37. How many were still missing? _____

c. Mel dropped 75 pencils. She picked up 57. How many are still on the floor? _____

d. Ajit needs 72 nails. He has 56. How many more does he need? _____

3 Complete the pattern in each box.

a.	**b.**	**c.**
$15 - 7 = 8$	$13 - 6 = $ _____	$11 - 5 = $ _____
$25 - 7 = $ _____	$23 - 6 = $ _____	_____ $- 5 = 16$
$35 - 7 = $ _____	$33 - $ _____ $= 27$	$31 - $ _____ $= 26$

d.	**e.**	**f.**
$12 - 7 = $ _____	$14 - 9 = $ _____	$16 - $ _____ $= 9$
$22 - $ _____ $= 15$	_____ $- 9 = 15$	$26 - 7 = $ _____
_____ $- 7 = 25$	$34 - 9 = $ _____	_____ $- 7 = 29$

4 Use the chart in question 1 to find the number that is 9 less than 32. _____

5 Eddie needs 27 nails. He has 18. Count backward to find how many more he needs.

_____

6 Complete the pattern. $17 - 9 = $ ___

$27 - $ ___ $= 18$

___ $- 9 = 28$

Checking Subtraction by Adding

1 Subtract. Check each answer by adding.

a.
```
  24  →  [    ]
 -13     +13
[    ]   [    ]
```

b.
```
  46  →  [    ]
 -34     +34
[    ]   [    ]
```

c.
```
  32  →  [    ]
 - 9     + 9
[    ]   [    ]
```

d.
```
  42  →  [    ]
 -16     +16
[    ]   [    ]
```

2 Complete each question. Check your answer in the box.

a.
```
  59  [    ]
 -36
```

b.
```
  74  [    ]
 -51
```

c.
```
  46  [    ]
 -37
```

d.
```
  52  [    ]
 -25
```

3 Use the information given on the sign to determine if the following distances are correct. If a distance is correct, write *correct* on the line. If a distance is incorrect, write the correct answer on the line. Check by adding.

Beach	5 miles
Restaurant	14 miles
Park	22 miles
Gas Station	55 miles

	From	To	Distance	Correct?
a.	Beach	Restaurant	9 miles	_____
b.	Restaurant	Gas Station	49 miles	_____
c.	Park	Gas Station	34 miles	_____
d.	Beach	Park	17 miles	_____

4 Subtract and check your answer.
```
  52  →  [    ]
 -29     +29
[    ]   [    ]
```

5 Solve. 41 – 17 = _____ Check. _____

6 Look at the sign. Is the distance from Vincent to Newton 24 miles? Check by adding. _____

Vincent	18 miles
Newton	42 miles

Subtraction Review

1 Complete the subtraction wheel.

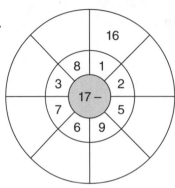

2 Charles has $24. He spends $15. How much does he have left? _____

3 Solve. 46 – 13 = _____. Hint: Remember to break 13 down into 10 and 3!

4 Yuko had 37 marbles. She gave away 6 and had 43 left.

    a. What is wrong with this story? _____

    _____

    b. How many marbles did Yuko really have left? _____

5 Amelia bought a calculator for $13 and a book for $83. If she had $100 to begin with, how much money did she have left? _____

6 Find four pairs of numbers with a difference of 37.

    _____   _____   _____   _____

7 Mark bought two computer games for $89 each. How much change will he get back from $200? _____

8 Write as many different subtraction equations as possible using the numbers 9, 11, and 20.

    _____

9 Subtract.   1,265 – 391 = _____

10 Write four number sentences that have a difference of 25.

    _____   _____   _____   _____

Multiplication with Modeling

1 Complete each number sentence.

a.

3 rows of 4 = _____

b. ○○○○○
○○○○○

2 rows of 5 = _____

c. ○○○○○
○○○○○
○○○○○

_____ rows of 5 = _____

d. ○○○○○○○
○○○○○○○

_____ rows of 7 = _____

e.

____ rows of ____ = ____

f. ☐☐☐☐☐

____ row of ____ = ____

2 Complete the number sentences.

a. 4 groups of 7 hats = _____

b. 9 groups of 2 fish = _____

c. 7 boys on a team. 6 teams. How many boys? _____

d. 8 nails in a packet. 4 packets. How many nails? _____

3 Answer *yes* or *no* to each of the statements.

a. 6×3 equals 3×6 _____

b. 3×9 equals $9 + 9 + 9$ _____

c. 5×2 equals 10×1 _____

d. 4×6 equals 3×8 _____

e. 5×7 equals $7 + 7 + 7 + 7 + 7$ _____

f. 8×9 equals 9×8 _____

4 Complete the number sentence.

○○○○○○
○○○○○○
○○○○○○   ____ rows of ____ = ____

5 Complete. 3 groups of 5 cups = _____

6 *Yes* or *no*?

4×6 equals $6 + 6 + 6 + 6$ _____

Multiplying by 2 and 4

1 Use the pictures to complete the number sentences.

a.

3 groups of 4 = _____

b.

7 groups of 4 = _____

c.

9 groups of 4 = _____

d.

_____ groups of 4 = 8

e.

_____ group of 4 = _____

f.

_____ groups of 4 = _____

2 Use the picture to complete the number sentences.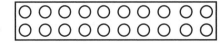

a. 4 × 2 = _____

b. 10 × 2 = _____

c. 7 × 2 = _____

d. _____ × 2 = 10

e. _____ × 2 = 16

f. _____ × 2 = 12

3 Study the pictures to complete the number sentences.

a.

5 × 4 = _____

b.

7 × 2 = _____

c.

10 × 2 = _____

d.

8 × 4 = _____

4 Complete the number sentence.

3 × 4 = _____

5 Use the array to complete the number sentence.

_____ × 2 = 18

6 Study the model and complete the number sentence.

3 × 2 = _____

1 Use the diagrams to complete the following number sentences.

a. △ △ △
△ △ △

6 groups of 1 = _____

b. ▯ ▯ ▯

3 groups of 0 = _____

c. △ △ △ △
△ △ △ △ △

9 groups of 1 = _____

d. ▯ ▯ ▯ ▯ ▯
▯ ▯ ▯ ▯ ▯

10 groups of 0 = _____

e.

5 groups of 4 = _____

f.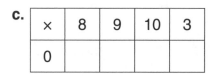

8 groups of 2 = _____

2 Complete the following tables.

a.

×	7	8	9	10
4				

b.

×	1	2	3	4
2				

c.

×	8	9	10	3
0				

d.

×	1	2	3	4
1				

e.

×	5	6	7	8
2				

f.

×	3	4	5	6
4				

3 Write each product on the line.

a. $2 \times 1 =$ _____ $= 1 \times 2$

b. $4 \times 0 =$ _____ $= 6 \times 0$

c. $3 \times 4 =$ _____ $= 6 \times 2$

d. $10 \times 2 =$ _____ $= 5 \times 4$

e. $4 \times 4 =$ _____ $= 8 \times 2$

f. $10 \times 1 =$ _____ $= 5 \times 2$

4 Complete the number sentence. ▯ ▯ ▯ ▯
▯ ▯ ▯ ▯

8 groups of 0 = _____

5 Complete the table.

×	7	8	9	10
1				

6 Complete the number sentence. $3 \times 2 =$ _____ $= 6 \times 1$

1 Use the diagrams to complete the number sentences.

a.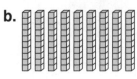

6 groups of 10 = _____

b.

9 groups of 10 = _____

c.

4 groups of 10 = _____

2 Use the picture to complete the number sentences.

a. $8 \times 5 =$ _____

b. $5 \times 5 =$ _____

c. $2 \times 5 =$ _____

d. _____ $\times 5 = 35$

e. _____ $\times 5 = 50$

f. _____ $\times 5 = 45$

3 Complete the tables.

a.

×	1	2	3	4
5				

b.

×	1	2	3	4
10				

c.

×	5	6	7	8	9
10					

d.

×	5	6	7	8	9
5					

4 Use the diagram to answer.

5 groups of 10 = _____

5 Use the picture below to complete the problem.

_____ $\times 5 = 60$

6 Complete the table.

×	10	11	12	13	14
5					

Multiplying by 3 and 6

1 Write a multiplication number sentence to describe each model.

a. ○ ○ ○
○ ○ ○
○ ○ ○

_____

b. ○ ○ ○ ○ ○ ○
○ ○ ○ ○ ○ ○
○ ○ ○ ○ ○ ○
○ ○ ○ ○ ○ ○

_____

c. ○ ○ ○ ○ ○ ○
○ ○ ○ ○ ○ ○
○ ○ ○ ○ ○ ○
○ ○ ○ ○ ○ ○
○ ○ ○ ○ ○ ○
○ ○ ○ ○ ○ ○

_____

d. ○ ○ ○
○ ○ ○
○ ○ ○
○ ○ ○
○ ○ ○
○ ○ ○
○ ○ ○
○ ○ ○
○ ○ ○
○ ○ ○
○ ○ ○
○ ○ ○

_____

2 Complete the problems.

a. $1 \times 6 =$ _____ $= 6 \times 1$

b. $10 \times 6 =$ _____ $=$ _____ $\times 10$

c. _____ $\times 6 =$ _____ $= 6 \times 5$

d. _____ $\times 6 = 54 = 6 \times$ _____

e. $8 \times 6 =$ _____ $=$ _____ $\times 8$

f. $3 \times 6 =$ _____ $=$ _____ $\times 3$

3 Complete the problems.

a. $5 \times 6 =$ _____

b. _____ $\times 3 = 18$

c. $9 \times 6 =$ _____

d. $5 \times$ _____ $= 15$

e. _____ $\times 6 = 42$

f. $9 \times 3 =$ _____

4 Write a multiplication number sentence to describe the model.

_____

5 Complete the problem. _____ $\times 3 =$ _____ $= 3 \times 6$

6 Complete the problem. $6 \times$ _____ $= 36$

Multiplying by 9

1 Use the picture to help answer the following questions.

○○○○○○○○○○
○○○○○○○○○○
○○○○○○○○○○
○○○○○○○○○○
○○○○○○○○○○
○○○○○○○○○○
○○○○○○○○○○
○○○○○○○○○○
○○○○○○○○○○

a. 3 groups of 9 = _____

b. 8 groups of 9 = _____

c. 2 columns of 9 = _____

d. 10 columns of 9 = _____

2 Write a multiplication expression for each multiple of **9** given below.

a. 27 = _____

b. 18 = _____

c. 63 = _____

d. 36 = _____

e. 9 = _____

f. 45 = _____

3 Complete the problems.

a. $9 \times 2 = 18 =$ _____ $\times 6$

b. $4 \times$ _____ $= 36 = 6 \times$ _____

c. $9 \times 10 =$ _____ $=$ _____ $\times 9$

d. _____ $\times 9 = 9 = 3 \times$ _____

e. $6 \times 9 =$ _____ $= 9 \times$ _____

f. _____ $\times 9 = 63 = 9 \times$ _____

4 Use the picture to answer the problem.

○○○○○○○○○○
○○○○○○○○○○
○○○○○○○○○○
○○○○○○○○○○
○○○○○○○○○○

5 groups of 9 = _____

5 Write a multiplication expression that has a product of 54. _____

6 Complete the problem. $3 \times$ _____ $=$ _____ $= 9 \times 1$

1 Use the models below to find each product.

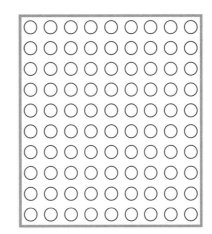

a. $7 \times 3 =$ _____

b. $9 \times 6 =$ _____

c. $5 \times 9 =$ _____

d. $6 \times 3 =$ _____

e. $4 \times 6 =$ _____

f. $2 \times 9 =$ _____

2 Find each product.

a. The product of 4 and 3 = _____

b. The product of 8 and 6 = _____

c. The product of 8 and 9 = _____

d. The product of 10 and 3 = _____

3 Fill in the blanks to make each equation true.

a. $3 \times 2 =$ _____ $=$ _____ $\times 1$

b. $6 \times$ _____ $= 36 = 9 \times$ _____

c. $3 \times$ _____ $= 24 = 6 \times$ _____

d. _____ $\times 6 = 18 = 2 \times$ _____

4 Use the model to find the product. $3 \times 4 =$ _____

5 Multiply. The product of 6 and 9 = _____.

6 Fill in the blanks to make the equation true. $4 \times$ _____ $= 36 =$ _____ $\times 6$

1 Complete.

    a. 6 groups of 8 = _____   **b.** 0 groups of 8 = _____

    c. 4 groups of 8 = _____   **d.** 2 groups of 8 = _____

2 Complete the equations.

    a. $1 \times 8 =$ _____   **b.** _____ $\times 8 = 32$

    c. _____ $\times 8 = 56$ **d.** $6 \times$ _____ $= 48$

3 Complete.

a.	**b.**	**c.**
8	8	5
× 2	× 8	× 8

d.	**e.**	**f.**
1 0	8	9
× 8	× 4	× 8

4 Complete.   7 groups of 8 = _____

5 Complete the problem.   _____ $\times 8 = 80$

6 Complete.   3

                   × 8

Multiplying by 2, 4, and 8

1 Use the models to find each product.

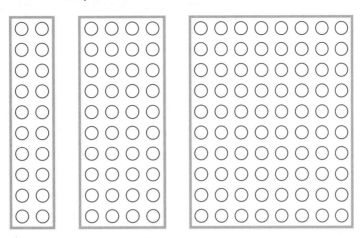

a. $7 \times 2 =$ _____

b. $7 \times 4 =$ _____

c. $3 \times 8 =$ _____

d. $6 \times 2 =$ _____

e. $5 \times 4 =$ _____

f. $6 \times 8 =$ _____

2 Find each product.

a. The product of 3 and 2 = _____.

b. The product of 8 and 4 = _____.

c. The product of 7 and 8 = _____.

d. The product of 9 and 2 = _____.

3 Fill in the blank(s) to make each equation true.

a. $4 \times 2 =$ _____ $= 8 \times 1$

b. $6 \times 4 =$ _____ $= 8 \times$ _____

c. $5 \times$ _____ $= 40 = 10 \times$ _____

d. $10 \times$ _____ $= 20 = 4 \times$ _____

e. $6 \times$ _____ $=$ _____ $= 4 \times 3$

f. $6 \times$ _____ $=$ _____ $= 3 \times 8$

4 Use the models to find the products.

a. $5 \times 4 =$ _____

b. $5 \times 2 =$ _____

5 Multiply. The product of 9 and 4 = _____.

6 Fill in the blanks to make the equation true. $4 \times$ _____ $= 16 =$ _____ $\times 2$

Multiplying by 7

1

January						
S	M	T	W	T	F	S
		1	2	3	4	5
6	7	8	9	10	11	12
13	14	15	16	17	18	19
20	21	22	23	24	25	26
27	28	29	30	31		

February						
S	M	T	W	T	F	S
					1	2
3	4	5	6	7	8	9
10	11	12	13	14	15	16
17	18	19	20	21	22	23
24	25	26	27	28		

March						
S	M	T	W	T	F	S
					1	2
3	4	5	6	7	8	9
10	11	12	13	14	15	16
17	18	19	20	21	22	23
24/31	25	26	27	28	29	30

There are seven days in a week. How many days are there in . . .

a. 3 weeks? _____

b. 5 weeks? _____

c. 6 weeks? _____

d. 4 weeks? _____

2 Complete.

a. 0 groups of 7 = _____

b. 6 groups of 7 = _____

c. 4 groups of 7 = _____

d. 10 groups of 7 = _____

3 Multiply.

a. $\begin{array}{r} 3 \\ \times\ 7 \\ \hline \end{array}$

b. $\begin{array}{r} 7 \\ \times\ 4 \\ \hline \end{array}$

c. $\begin{array}{r} 8 \\ \times\ 7 \\ \hline \end{array}$

d. $\begin{array}{r} 7 \\ \times\ 2 \\ \hline \end{array}$

4 How many days are there in 7 weeks? _____

5 Complete. 9 groups of 7 = _____

6 Multiply. $\begin{array}{r} 7 \\ \times\ 7 \\ \hline \end{array}$

Multiplication Tables

1 Complete the problems.

    a. 6 groups of 4 = _____

    b. 4 groups of 2 = _____

    c. 5 groups of 5 = _____

    d. 3 groups of 8 = _____

2 Multiply.

    a. $1 \times 5 =$ _____

    b. $10 \times 3 =$ _____

    c. $2 \times 10 =$ _____

    d. $6 \times 7 =$ _____

3 Multiply.

    a.

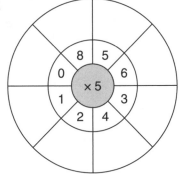

    b.

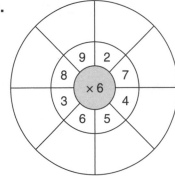

    c.

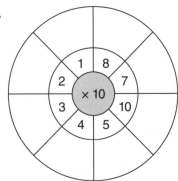

    d.

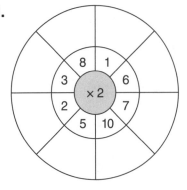

4 Complete. 10 groups of 8 = _____

5 Multiply. $4 \times 6 =$ _____

6 Multiply.

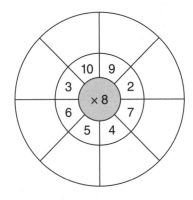

Square Numbers

1 Complete the problems for the square numbers.

> **a.** $1^2 = 1 \times 1 =$ _____   •

> **b.** $2^2 = 2 \times 2 =$ _____

> **c.** $3^2 = 3 \times 3 =$ _____

> **d.** $4^2 = 4 \times 4 =$ _____

> **e.** $5^2 = 5 \times 5 =$ _____

> **f.** $6^2 = 6 \times 6 =$ _____

2 Finish drawing the large **squares** using the bold black lines as guides. Calculate the area of each large square.

a.

b.

c.

area = _____ squares   area = _____ squares   area = _____ squares

3 Are the following numbers square numbers? Write *yes* or *no* on the line.

a. 25 _____   **b.** 49 _____   **c.** 50 _____

d. 100 _____   **e.** 75 _____   **f.** 81 _____

4 Complete the problem for the square number.

$7^2 = 7 \times 7 =$ _____

5 Finish drawing the square. Calculate its area.

area = _____ squares

6 Is 99 a square number? _____

Multiples

1

1	2	3	4	5	6	7	8	9	10
11	12	13	14	15	16	17	18	19	20
21	22	23	24	25	26	27	28	29	30
31	32	33	34	35	36	37	38	39	40
41	42	43	44	45	46	47	48	49	50

a. Circle each multiple of 2.   **b.** Shade the multiples of 4.   **c.** Put an x on the multiples of 8.

d. Are the multiples of 2, 4, and 8 related? _____

Why do you think they are related? _____

e. Why is the number 50 not crossed out? _____

2 List the first ten multiples of . . .

a. | 2 | | | | | | | | | |

b. | 3 | | | | | | | | | |

c. | 9 | | | | | | | | | |

d. | 5 | | | | | | | | | |

e. | 6 | | | | | | | | | |

f. | 7 | | | | | | | | | |

3 Shade the multiples of the number in the center.

a.
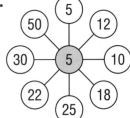

b.
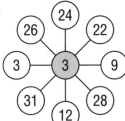

c.
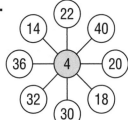

d.
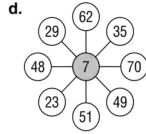

4 On the completed chart from question 1, why was the number 30 not shaded?

_____

5 List the first ten multiples of . . .

| 10 | | | | | | | | | |

6 Shade the multiples of 8.

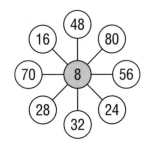

Multiplication Review

1 Write all of the different multiplication expressions possible that have a product of 12.

_____   _____   _____

_____   _____   _____

Complete the multiplication wheels.

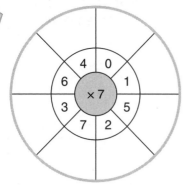 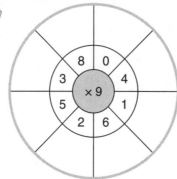 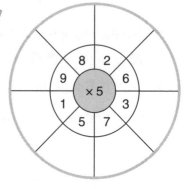

5 In the box below, *circle* the multiples of 2 and *shade* the multiples of 4.

```
 1   2   3   4   5   6   7   8   9  10
11  12  13  14  15  16  17  18  19  20
21  22  23  24  25  26  27  28  29  30
31  32  33  34  35  36  37  38  39  40
```

What did you discover about the multiples of two and four?

_____

6 What is the total cost of 8 movie tickets if tickets are $6 each? _____

7 Fill in the blanks. $4 \times$ _____ $= 36 =$ _____ $\times 6$

8 List all the square numbers up to 100.

_____

Factors are numbers that when multiplied together give another number (product). For example, 2 and 3 are factors of 6 since 2 x 3 = 6. List all the factors of the following numbers.

9 12: _____

10 18: _____

1 Use the pictures to show how you could share the cookies in each group.

a. 10 shared by 2

b. 12 shared by 3

c. 9 shared by 3

d. 6 shared by 2

e. 16 shared by 4

f. 8 shared by 4

2 Complete.

a. 21 shared among 3 = _____   **b.** 12 shared among 6 = _____

c. 18 shared among 9 = _____   **d.** 20 shared among 5 = _____

3 10 pieces of toast . . .

a. shared by 5 = _____

b. shared by 2 = _____

c. shared by 3 = _____ and _____ left over

d. shared by 4 = _____ and _____ left over

4 Use the picture to show how to share 12 cookies by 6 people.

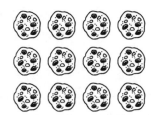

5 Complete: 25 shared among 5 = _____

6 9 cups shared by 4 = _____ and _____ left over

Division as Repeated Subtraction

1 How many groups of 2 could be made from each of the following groups? Find the answer by crossing out 2 items at a time.

a.  _____

b.  _____

c.  _____

d.  _____

2 There are 12 apples in the bowl.

    a. How many times can I take 2 apples? _____ times

    b. How many times can I take 4 apples? _____ times

    c. How many times can I take 12 apples? _____ times

    d. How many times can I take 1 apple? _____ times

3   **a.** How many times can I take 5 candles from 10? _____

    b. How many times can I take 6 books from 30? _____

    c. How many times can I take 4 balls from 20? _____

    d. How many times can I take 2 pens from 24? _____

4 How many groups of 2 could be made from  ? _____

5 There are 15 oranges in the bowl.
How many times can I take 3 oranges? _____

6 How many times can I take 4 grapes from 16? _____

Division

1 Use the models to answer the following division questions.

a. ○ ○
○ ○
○ ○ $6 \div 3 =$ _____

b.
○ ○ ○ ○
○ ○ ○ ○ $8 \div 4 =$ _____

c. ○ ○ ○ ○ ○
○ ○ ○ ○ ○
○ ○ ○ ○ ○ $15 \div 3 =$ _____

d. ○ ○ ○
○ ○ ○
○ ○ ○ $9 \div 3 =$ _____

2 Draw models for the division number sentences.

a. $9 \div 3 = 3$ **b.** $10 \div 2 = 5$ **c.** $9 \div 1 = 9$

d. $14 \div 2 = 7$ **e.** $16 \div 4 = 4$ **f.** $12 \div 6 = 2$

3 Answer the questions.

a. How many 5s in 25? _____   **b.** How many 3s in 21? _____

c. How many 10s in 100? _____   **d.** How many 8s in 48? _____

4 Use this model to find the answer to $16 \div 8 =$ _____.

○ ○ ○ ○
○ ○ ○ ○
○ ○ ○ ○
○ ○ ○ ○

5 Draw a model for the division equation.

$14 \div 7 = 2$

6 How many 4s in 28? _____

Division with Remainders

1 Circle the following:

a. groups of 3 circles

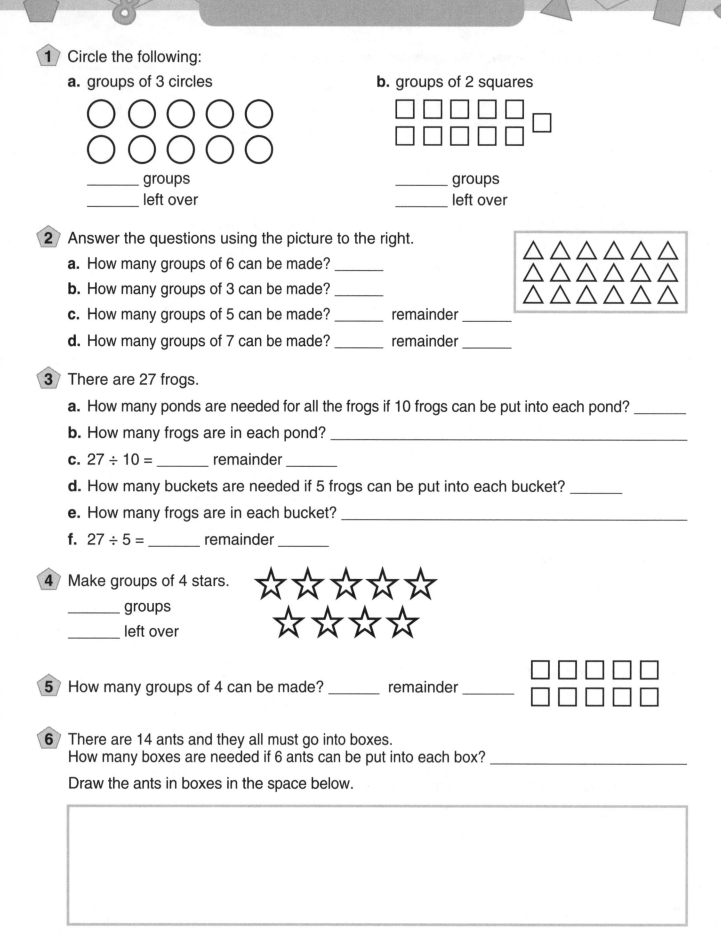

_____ groups
_____ left over

b. groups of 2 squares

_____ groups
_____ left over

2 Answer the questions using the picture to the right.

a. How many groups of 6 can be made? _____

b. How many groups of 3 can be made? _____

c. How many groups of 5 can be made? _____ remainder _____

d. How many groups of 7 can be made? _____ remainder _____

3 There are 27 frogs.

a. How many ponds are needed for all the frogs if 10 frogs can be put into each pond? _____

b. How many frogs are in each pond? _____

c. 27 ÷ 10 = _____ remainder _____

d. How many buckets are needed if 5 frogs can be put into each bucket? _____

e. How many frogs are in each bucket? _____

f. 27 ÷ 5 = _____ remainder _____

4 Make groups of 4 stars.

_____ groups
_____ left over

5 How many groups of 4 can be made? _____ remainder _____

6 There are 14 ants and they all must go into boxes.
How many boxes are needed if 6 ants can be put into each box? _____

Draw the ants in boxes in the space below.

More Division Practice

1 Use the given multiplication fact to solve each division problem.

a. $5 \times 9 = 45$

$9\overline{)45}$

b. $8 \times 7 = 56$

$8\overline{)56}$

c. $6 \times 7 = 42$

$7\overline{)42}$

d. $4 \times 8 = 32$

$4\overline{)32}$

e. $9 \times 9 = 81$

$9\overline{)81}$

f. $8 \times 10 = 80$

$10\overline{)80}$

2 Complete.

a. $40 \div 10 =$ _____

b. $64 \div 8 =$ _____

c. $35 \div 7 =$ _____

d. $9 \div 4 =$ ____ **r** ____

e. $14 \div 5 =$ ____ **r** ____

f. $20 \div 8 =$ ____ **r** ____

3 **a.** Divide 30 marbles into 5 groups. _____ marbles per group

b. Share 32 chocolates among 8 ladies. _____ chocolates per lady

c. Divide 16 dogs into 2 groups. _____ dogs per group

d. Share 20 candies between 6 children. _____ candies per child **r** _____

e. Divide 22 fish into 7 fish bowls. _____ fish per bowl **r** _____

f. Share 18 snacks between 4 boys. _____ snacks per boy **r** _____

4 Use the multiplication fact $9 \times 8 = 72$ to solve the division problem.

$8\overline{)72}$

5 Complete. $24 \div 8 =$ _____

6 Divide 17 toy trucks among 5 girls. _____ trucks per girl **r** _____

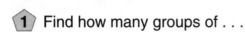

Multiplication and Division

1 Find how many groups of . . .

    a. 4 buttons can be made from 24 buttons. _____

    b. 3 hats can be made from 15 hats. _____

    c. 3 fish can be made from 6 fish. _____

    d. 2 balls can be made from 10 balls. _____

2 Use the multiplication number sentence at the beginning of each row to complete the two division sentences.

    a. $5 \times 3 = 15$ $15 \div 3 =$ _____ $15 \div 5 =$ _____

    b. $6 \times 4 = 24$ $24 \div 4 =$ _____ $24 \div 6 =$ _____

    c. $10 \times 9 = 90$ $90 \div 9 =$ _____ $90 \div 10 =$ _____

    d. $8 \times 7 = 56$ $56 \div 7 =$ _____ $56 \div 8 =$ _____

3 Use the division number sentence at the beginning of each row to complete the two multiplication sentences.

    a. $24 \div 6 = 4$ _____ $\times 6 = 24$ $6 \times$ _____ $= 24$

    b. $45 \div 5 = 9$ _____ $\times 5 = 45$ _____ $\times 9 = 45$

    c. $18 \div 3 = 6$ $6 \times$ _____ $= 18$ $3 \times$ _____ $= 18$

    d. $70 \div 7 = 10$ _____ $\times 7 = 70$ $7 \times$ _____ $= 70$

4 There are 18 golf balls. Find how many groups of 6 golf balls can be made. _____

5 Use the first number sentence to complete the other two.

         $7 \times 5 = 35$ $35 \div 7 =$ _____ $35 \div 5 =$ _____

6 Use the first number sentence to complete the other two.

         $63 \div 9 = 7$ _____ $\times 9 = 63$ _____ $\times 7 = 63$

1 Write as many different division expressions with quotients of 12 that you can.

_____

_____

2 Scarlet bought 22 apples. She put the same number of apples in each of 5 fruit bowls. How many apples did Scarlet put in each fruit bowl? _____ How many were left over? _____

3 If Amy buys only 5¢ stamps, how many stamps could she buy for 40¢? _____

4 20 balls are packaged into boxes of 6. In the space below, draw a picture showing the balls in the boxes. If any balls are left over, draw them outside of the boxes.

5 **BINGO!** Cross off all the winning numbers to find which row wins. **Winning Row:** _____

A	20	42	10	36
B	4	2	6	3
C	16	8	7	32

a. 5 x 2   **b.** 4 x 4   **c.** 24 ÷ 4   **d.** 40 ÷ 10

e. 6 x 7   **f.** 6 ÷ 2   **g.** 4 x 8   **h.** 16 ÷ 8

6 Write four division problems with quotients of 5.

_____

7 Write two multiplication and two division facts that equal 10.

multiplication: _____ and _____

division: _____ and _____

8 Complete the division wheel.

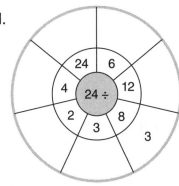

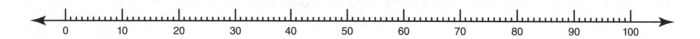

0   10   20   30   40   50   60   70   80   90   100

1 Use the number line to find the sums.

a. 32 + 19 = _____   **b.** 31 + 28 = _____   **c.** 36 + 17 = _____

2 Use the number line to find the differences.

a. 50 − 13 = _____   **b.** 29 − 7 = _____   **c.** 43 − 15 = _____

3 Use the number line to find the products.

a. 5 × 3 = _____   **b.** 4 × 6 = _____   **c.** 7 × 4 = _____

4 Use the number line to find the quotients.

a. 20 ÷ 5 = _____   **b.** 18 ÷ 9 = _____   **c.** 21 ÷ 7 = _____

5 Use the number line to solve: 79 + 14 = _____

6 Use the number line to solve: 94 − 16 = _____

7 Use the number line to solve: 3 × 8 = _____

8 Use the number line to solve: 28 ÷ 4 = _____

Inverse Operations

1 Check the addition facts by using subtraction.

    a. $8 + 6 = 14$ $14 -$ _____ $=$ _____   **b.** $9 + 15 = 24$ $24 -$ _____ $=$ _____

    c. $24 + 7 = 31$ $31 -$ _____ $=$ _____   **d.** $17 + 8 = 25$ $25 -$ _____ $=$ _____

2 Check the subtraction facts by using addition.

    a. $14 - 6 = 8$ $8 +$ _____ $=$ _____   **b.** $21 - 8 = 13$ $13 +$ _____ $=$ _____

    c. $25 - 19 = 6$ $6 +$ _____ $=$ _____   **d.** $36 - 17 = 19$ $19 +$ _____ $=$ _____

3 Write a division fact from each multiplication fact.

    a. $7 \times 5 = 35$ $35 \div$ _____ $=$ _____   **b.** $9 \times 3 = 27$ $27 \div$ _____ $=$ _____

    c. $4 \times 9 = 36$ $36 \div$ _____ $=$ _____   **d.** $8 \times 6 = 48$ $48 \div$ _____ $=$ _____

4 Write a multiplication fact from each division fact.

    a. $16 \div 4 = 4$ $4 \times$ _____ $=$ _____   **b.** $21 \div 7 = 3$ $3 \times$ _____ $=$ _____

    c. $18 \div 6 = 3$ $3 \times$ _____ $=$ _____   **d.** $20 \div 4 = 5$ $5 \times$ _____ $=$ _____

5 Check the addition fact by using subtraction.

            $29 + 17 = 46$ $46 -$ _____ $=$ _____

6 Check the subtraction fact by using addition.

            $24 - 16 = 8$ $8 +$ _____ $=$ _____

7 Write a division fact from the multiplication fact.

            $8 \times 7 = 56$ $56 \div$ _____ $=$ _____

8 Write a multiplication fact from the division fact.

            $27 \div 9 = 3$ $3 \times$ _____ $=$ _____

Which Order?

1 Add the sets of numbers.

    a. 6 + 4 = _____   4 + 6 = _____   **b.** 10 + 12 = _____   12 + 10 = _____

    c. 6 + 9 = _____   9 + 6 = _____   **d.** 8 + 5 = _____   5 + 8 = _____

2 Multiply the sets of numbers.

    a. 3 × 6 = _____   6 × 3 = _____   **b.** 4 × 2 = _____   2 × 4 = _____

    c. 6 × 7 = _____   7 × 6 = _____   **d.** 5 × 8 = _____   8 × 5 = _____

3 Rewrite each number sentence to make it easier to solve. Then solve.

    a. 6 + 7 + 4 = _____   **b.** 18 + 4 + 2 = _____

    c. 17 + 6 + 3 = _____   **d.** 7 + 8 + 3 = _____

4 Add the numbers below.

            18 + 3 = _____   3 + 18 = _____

5 Multiply the numbers below.

            8 × 6 = _____   6 × 8 = _____

6 In the box below, rewrite the sum 14 + 9 + 6 to make it easier to solve. Then solve.

Bingo!

1 Mark off the sums to find the winning row. **Winning Row:** _____

A	17	4	6	15
B	3	8	11	2
C	10	16	7	14

a. $4 + 3$ **b.** $8 + 7$ **c.** $10 + 6$

d. $3 + 11$ **e.** $6 + 5$ **f.** $1 + 9$

2 Mark off the differences to find the winning row. **Winning Row:** _____

A	5	12	8	4
B	6	10	1	2
C	3	11	7	9

a. $8 - 7$ **b.** $11 - 5$ **c.** $15 - 7$

d. $16 - 9$ **e.** $7 - 5$ **f.** $18 - 8$

3 Mark off the products to find the winning row. **Winning Row:** _____

A	6	16	15	4
B	10	14	9	8
C	2	18	12	20

a. 4×5 **b.** 3×6 **c.** 2×1

d. 5×2 **e.** 3×3 **f.** 4×3

4 Mark off the quotients to find the winning row. **Winning Row:** _____

A	10	2	8	9
B	12	3	5	6
C	1	16	4	7

a. $16 \div 2$ **b.** $12 \div 3$ **c.** $20 \div 2$

d. $14 \div 7$ **e.** $18 \div 6$ **f.** $9 \div 1$

5 Mark off the solutions to find the winning row. **Winning Row:** _____

A	4	8	12	7
B	6	10	2	15
C	9	1	3	13

a. 3×1 **b.** $11 - 10$ **c.** $16 \div 4$

d. $14 \div 2$ **e.** $3 + 5$ **f.** 2×6

1 Supply the missing number to make each equation true.

a. $8 +$ _____ $= 14$ b. $35 +$ _____ $= 50$

c. $46 -$ _____ $= 12$ d. $17 -$ _____ $= 9$

2 Supply the missing number to make each equation true.

a. $7 \times$ _____ $= 28$ b. $6 \times$ _____ $= 30$

c. $24 \div$ _____ $= 6$ d. $9 \div$ _____ $= 3$

3 Use a **+, −, ×,** or **÷** symbol to make each number sentence correct.

a. $4 \boxed{} 7 = 11$ b. $4 \boxed{} 3 = 12$

c. $18 \boxed{} 12 = 6$ d. $13 \boxed{} 11 = 24$

4 Supply the missing number to make the equation true.

$$25 + \underline{\hspace{2cm}} = 47$$

5 Supply the missing number to make the equation true.

a. _____ $\times 3 = 21$ b. $80 \div$ _____ $= 8$

6 Use a **+, −, ×,** or **÷** symbol to make $15 \boxed{} 5 = 3$ correct.

Operations Review

1 Fill in the blank. $35 - \underline{\hspace{1cm}} = 12$

2 Fill in the blank. $19 \underline{\hspace{1cm}} 6 = 13$

3 Fill in the blank. $13 \underline{\hspace{1cm}} 11 = 24$

4 Write a division fact related to 3 x 9 = 27. _____

5 Complete.

a. $6 \times 9 = \underline{\hspace{1cm}}$ $\underline{\hspace{1cm}} \div 6 = 9$ **b.** $9 \times \underline{\hspace{1cm}} = 54$ $\underline{\hspace{1cm}} \div 9 = 6$

c. $9 + 9 + 9 + \underline{\hspace{1cm}} + \underline{\hspace{1cm}} + \underline{\hspace{1cm}} = 54$

6 Mark off the answers on the BINGO cards to find the winning card. Circle the winning card.

A

11	26	60
10	24	100
28	3	110

B

2	9	0
19	16	13
5	6	1

C

12	35	17
46	8	7
4	36	49

15 – 4	49 ÷ 7	72 ÷ 8	8 x 2
100 + 10	4 x 6	6 + 6	21 + 15
15 + 2	9 – 8	36 – 8	20 – 12
20 ÷ 10	25 ÷ 5	20 ÷ 2	5 x 12
8 x 0	2 x 2	9 + 37	20 + 15
17 + 9	100 – 87	60 – 11	8 – 5

7 Check the addition facts by using subtraction.

a. 26 + 5 = 31   31 – _____ = _____   **b.** 35 + 8 = 43   43 – _____ = _____

8 Check the subtraction facts by using addition.

a. 37 – 28 = 9   9 + _____ = _____   **b.** 23 – 6 = 17   17 + _____ = _____

9 Write a division fact related to each multiplication fact.

a. 2 x 9 = 18   18 ÷ _____ = _____   **b.** 3 x 10 = 30   30 ÷ _____ = _____

10 Write a multiplication fact related to each division fact.

a. 42 ÷ 6 = 7   7 x _____ = _____   **b.** 50 ÷ 5 = 10   10 x _____ = _____

Rules for Patterns

1 Continue each pattern by following the rule.

    a. Add 5: 25, _____, _____, _____

    b. Subtract 10: 100, _____, _____, _____

    c. Multiply by 2: 4, _____, _____, _____

    d. Add 8: 20, _____, _____, _____

2 Write a rule for each pattern.

    a. 2, 4, 6, 8 _____

    b. 20, 17, 14, 11 _____

    c. 10, 20, 30, 40 _____

    d. 9, 15, 21, 27 _____

3 Write the rule for the number of dots used in each pattern. Draw the next set of dots in each pattern.

    a. ● ●, ● ●/● ●, ● ●/● ●/● ●, _____

    _____

    b. ● ●, ● ●/● ●, ● ●/● ●/● ●, _____

    _____

    c. ●, ● ●, ● ●/● ●, ● ● ● ●, _____

    _____

    d. ●/● ●, ● ●/● ●, ● ●/● ● ●, _____

    _____

4 Continue the pattern of adding 6.   5, 11, _____, _____, _____

5 Write a rule.   5; 50; 500; 5,000 _____

6 Write the rule for the number of dots used. Draw the next set of dots in the pattern.

    ●, ●/● ●, ●/● ●/● ● ●, ●/● ●/● ● ●/● ● ● ●, _____

_____

_____

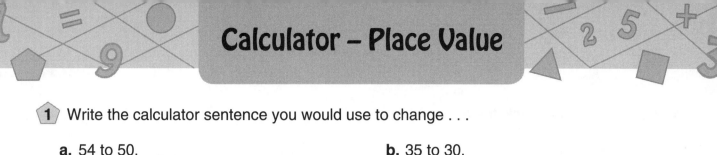

Calculator – Place Value

1 Write the calculator sentence you would use to change . . .

a. 54 to 50.

_____

b. 35 to 30.

_____

c. 230 to 236.

_____

d. 180 to 187.

_____

2 Write the calculator sentence you would use to change . . .

a. 86 to 6.

_____

b. 49 to 9.

_____

c. 508 to 558.

_____

d. 106 to 186.

_____

3 Write the calculator sentence you would use to change . . .

a. 427 to 27.

_____

b. 960 to 60.

_____

c. 20 to 120.

_____

d. 73 to 473.

_____

4 Write the calculator sentence you would use to change . . .

a. 1,426 to 426.

_____

b. 2,385 to 385.

_____

c. 160 to 5,160.

_____

d. 291 to 3,291.

_____

5 Write the calculator sentence you would use to change 419 to 410. _____

6 Write the calculator sentence you would use to change 906 to 946. _____

7 Write the calculator sentence you would use to change 73 to 573. _____

8 Write the calculator sentence you would use to change 491 to 6,491. _____

Calculator – Addition and Subtraction

1 Using a calculator, find the answer to each problem.

    a. 438 + 279 = _____   **b.** 562 + 893 = _____

    c. 479 – 389 = _____   **d.** 1,254 – 879 = _____

2 Using a calculator, find the answer to each problem.

    a. add 529 and 678 _____

    b. 326 minus 198 _____

    c. the difference between 812 and 485 _____

    d. the sum of 1,276 and 987 _____

3 Write a calculator sentence for each problem and find the answer.

    a. Sophie has 324 stamps and 479 cards. How many items does she have?

    _____

    b. Neil had 441 nails but used 279. How many did he have left?

    _____

    c. Kim picked 1,424 strawberries. She gave away 956. How many are left?

    _____

    d. Josh counted 275 blocks in one tub and 349 in another. What was the total number of blocks?

    _____

4 Use a calculator to find the answer. 2,926 + 1,462 = _____

5 Use a calculator to find the answer. 6,426 – 2,872 = _____

6 Use a calculator to find the sum of 621 and 1,856. _____

7 George needed 945 bricks to build a wall. He had 489 already. Write a calculator sentence to find how many more bricks were needed. Then solve.

_____

Calculator – Multiplication and Division

1 Using a calculator, find the answer to each problem.

    a. $33 \times 9 =$ _____   **b.** $48 \times 3 =$ _____   **c.** $110 \times 4 =$ _____

    d. $510 \div 5 =$ _____   **e.** $102 \div 3 =$ _____   **f.** $198 \div 2 =$ _____

2 Using a calculator, find the answer to each problem.

    a. 8 times 91 _____   **b.** 6 multiplied by 52 _____

    c. 9 groups of 14 _____   **d.** 126 divided by 3 _____

    e. How many 9s are there in 171? _____   **f.** How many groups of 8 in 136? _____

3 Write a calculator sentence for each problem and find the answer.

    a. Ben has 12 boxes of 15 apples. How many apples in total?

    _____

    b. David has 25 boxes of 35 matches. How many matches all together?

    _____

    c. Sue needs to put 198 brochures into 6 boxes. How many brochures in each box?

    _____

    d. Chris has 136 nails to put in 4 buckets. How many nails in each bucket?

    _____

4 Use a calculator to find the answers.

    a. $412 \times 7 =$ _____   **b.** $195 \div 5 =$ _____

5 Use a calculator to find the answer.

    How many groups of 4 are there in 424? _____

6 Write a calculator sentence and find the answer. There are 9 classes of 25 students at school. How many students are at the school?

_____

Fraction Names

1 Complete.

     a. $\frac{2}{3}$ is _____ out of 3 equal parts.

     b. $\frac{1}{4}$ is _____ out of 4 equal parts.

     c. $\frac{6}{8}$ is _____ out of _____ equal parts.

     d. $\frac{3}{5}$ is _____ out of _____ equal parts.

2 Write the fractions.

     a. two fifths _____

     b. seven eighths _____

     c. four sixths _____

     d. three tenths _____

     e. one third _____

     f. three fourths _____

3 Write the fractions in words.

     a. $\frac{1}{2}$ _____

     b. $\frac{4}{5}$ _____

     c. $\frac{3}{8}$ _____

     d. $\frac{2}{3}$ _____

4 Complete. $\frac{5}{8}$ is _____ out of _____ equal parts.

5 Write the fraction *two sixths* as a number. _____

6 Write the fraction $\frac{1}{6}$ in words. _____

Naming Fractions

1 What part of each of the following figures has been shaded?

    a.   **b.** 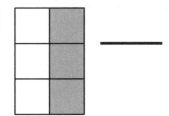   **c.**   **d.**

2 Color part of each shape to match the given fraction.

    a. 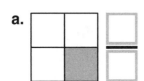 $\dfrac{1}{2}$ **b.** 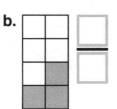 $\dfrac{3}{4}$ **c.**  $\dfrac{5}{8}$ **d.** 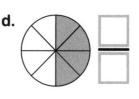 $\dfrac{3}{6}$

3 Write another fraction name for the shaded part, other than the one given.

    a. $\dfrac{3}{6}$ 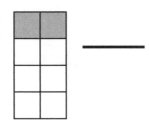 _____   **b.** $\dfrac{2}{2}$ 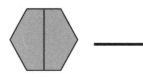 _____

    c. $\dfrac{2}{8}$ 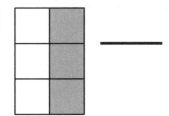 _____   **d.** $\dfrac{2}{6}$ 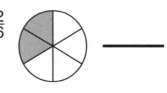 _____

4 What part of has been shaded? _____

5 Color part of 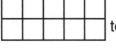 to show $\dfrac{3}{10}$.

6 Write another name for the shaded part of other than $\dfrac{4}{4}$. _____

Comparing Fractions

1 Circle the greater fraction.

a. $\frac{1}{4}$ or $\frac{2}{4}$

b. $\frac{4}{6}$ or $\frac{5}{6}$

c. $\frac{2}{3}$ or $\frac{1}{3}$

d. 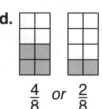 $\frac{4}{8}$ or $\frac{2}{8}$

2 Order the sets of fractions from *least* to *greatest*.

a. $\frac{1}{4}$, $\frac{4}{4}$, $\frac{2}{4}$, $\frac{3}{4}$

b. $\frac{2}{5}$, $\frac{4}{5}$, $\frac{1}{5}$, $\frac{3}{5}$

_____

_____

c. $\frac{4}{6}$, $\frac{2}{6}$, $\frac{3}{6}$, $\frac{6}{6}$

d. $\frac{3}{10}$, $\frac{9}{10}$, $\frac{7}{10}$, $\frac{5}{10}$

_____

_____

3 Circle the fraction that is less.

a. $\frac{2}{10}$ or $\frac{9}{10}$

b. $\frac{3}{4}$ or $\frac{1}{4}$

c. $\frac{4}{5}$ or $\frac{2}{5}$

d. $\frac{3}{3}$ or $\frac{1}{3}$

4 Circle the greatest fraction. 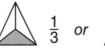 $\frac{1}{3}$ or $\frac{2}{3}$

5 Order the fractions $\frac{1}{5}$, $\frac{4}{5}$, $\frac{3}{5}$, and $\frac{5}{5}$ from *least* to *greatest*. _____

6 Circle the fraction that is less: $\frac{3}{4}$ or $\frac{1}{4}$.

Fractions of a Collection

1 Circle the given part of each collection and fill in the blank.

a. $\frac{1}{2}$ of 6 apples = _____ apples

b. $\frac{1}{4}$ of 8 strawberries = _____ strawberries

c. $\frac{1}{3}$ of 9 bananas = _____ bananas

d. $\frac{1}{8}$ of 8 cherries = _____ cherry

2 Draw a picture to show each of the following.

a. $\frac{1}{2}$ of 8 tennis balls	**b.** $\frac{1}{4}$ of 12 basketballs
c. $\frac{1}{10}$ of 20 golf balls	**d.** $\frac{1}{8}$ of 16 baseballs

3 Find the fraction of each collection.

a. $\frac{1}{4}$ of 16 triangles = _____

b. $\frac{1}{2}$ of 10 squares = _____

c. $\frac{1}{3}$ of 6 circles = _____

d. $\frac{1}{5}$ of 5 trapezoids = _____

4 Find $\frac{1}{5}$ of 15 cookies.

5 Draw a picture in the box to show $\frac{1}{2}$ of 14 balls.

6 Find $\frac{1}{3}$ of 12 diamonds. _____

Equivalent Fractions

1 Color part of each shape to match the given fraction. Then write an *equivalent* fraction to represent the part you colored.

a. $\frac{1}{2}$ _____

b. $\frac{1}{2}$ _____

c. $\frac{1}{2}$ _____

d. $\frac{1}{4}$ _____

e. $\frac{1}{4}$ _____

f. $\frac{1}{4}$ _____

2 Draw a line from each fraction in the top row to its equivalent fraction in the bottom row.

a. $\frac{2}{8}$ **b.** $\frac{1}{2}$ **c.** $\frac{1}{5}$ **d.** $\frac{3}{4}$

$\frac{2}{10}$ $\frac{6}{8}$ $\frac{1}{4}$ $\frac{5}{10}$

3 Write *true* or *false* for each statement.

a. $\frac{1}{2} = \frac{3}{4}$ _____   **b.** $\frac{5}{10} = \frac{1}{2}$ _____

c. $\frac{3}{4} = \frac{6}{8}$ _____   **d.** $\frac{2}{5} = \frac{4}{10}$ _____

4 Color part of ⬜ to show $\frac{1}{2}$. According to what you shaded, $\frac{1}{2} =$ _____.

5 Find the equivalent fractions. Draw lines from the fraction in the top row to its equivalent fraction in the bottom row.

a. $\frac{1}{4}$ **b.** $\frac{2}{10}$ **c.** $\frac{2}{3}$

$\frac{4}{6}$ $\frac{2}{8}$ $\frac{1}{5}$

6 Write *true* or *false*. $\frac{9}{10} = \frac{3}{5}$ _____

1 Draw a picture in the box to show eight tenths.

2 Is this shaded fraction  equal to this shaded fraction 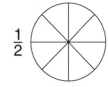? _____

3 Draw a picture to show $\frac{3}{4}$ of a circle.

4 Color the named fraction in each of the divided circles.

Circle the pizza that does not have the same amount colored as the other pizzas.

5 Circle the fraction that is *less*. $\frac{1}{8}$ *or* $\frac{3}{8}$

6 Polly scored $\frac{1}{8}$ of the 16 points scored in the basketball game. How many points did Polly score?

_____

7 There were 20 cookies on the tray. Al took $\frac{1}{4}$ of the cookies. How many cookies *were left* on the tray?

_____

8 True or false? $\frac{1}{2} = \frac{3}{4}$ _____

Circle the fractions that are equal (equivalent) in each row. Check carefully.

9 $\frac{2}{8}$ $\frac{1}{2}$ $\frac{1}{4}$

10 $\frac{2}{3}$ $\frac{4}{6}$ $\frac{6}{9}$

Hundredths

1 What part of each hundredths square has been colored? Write your answer as a fraction.

a. 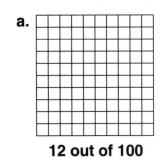 _____

b. 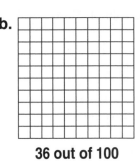 _____

c. 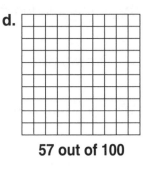 _____

2 Color the hundredths square to match the named part.

a.

12 out of 100

b.

36 out of 100

c.

23 out of 100

d.

57 out of 100

3 Circle the greater fraction in each pair.

a. $\frac{7}{100}$ *or* $\frac{17}{100}$
b. $\frac{39}{100}$ *or* $\frac{26}{100}$
c. $\frac{97}{100}$ *or* $\frac{66}{100}$
d. $\frac{56}{100}$ *or* $\frac{60}{100}$

4 What part of the hundredths square has been colored? Write the answer as a fraction.

 _____

5 Color $\frac{47}{100}$ on the hundredths square.

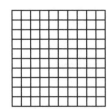

6 Circle the greater fraction in the pair.
$\frac{9}{100}$ $\frac{91}{100}$

Tenths

1 Use decimals to write each of the following fractions.

    a. five tenths _____

    b. nine tenths _____

    c. seven tenths _____

    d. three tenths _____

2 Write the decimal for each fraction.

    a. $\dfrac{1}{10}$ _____

    b. $\dfrac{4}{10}$ _____

    c. $\dfrac{3}{10}$ _____

    d. $\dfrac{6}{10}$ _____

3 Write the fraction for each decimal.

    a. 0.6 _____

    b. 0.3 _____

    c. 1.5 _____

    d. 1.2 _____

4 Use a decimal to write 4 tenths. _____

5 Write the decimal for $1\dfrac{7}{10}$. _____

6 Write the fraction.   0.7 _____

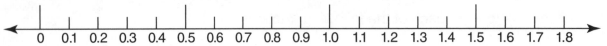

1 Start at . . .

    a. 0.5 and go forward 0.1. _____   **b.** 0.5 and go forward 0.2. _____

    c. 0.5 and go forward 0.4. _____   **d.** 0.5 and go forward 0.5. _____

2 Start at . . .

    a. 0.9 and go backward 0.1. _____   **b.** 0.9 and go backward 0.2. _____

    c. 0.9 and go backward 0.4. _____   **d.** 0.9 and go backward 0.8. _____

3 Start at 1.5.

    a. Go backward 0.4. _____   **b.** Then go forward 0.7. _____

    c. Then go backward 0.2. _____   **d.** Then go backward 0.1. _____

4 Start at 0.6 and go forward 0.3. _____

5 Start at 0.6 and go backward 0.4. _____

6 Start at 0.4. Go forward 0.2. Then go backward 0.3. _____

Decimals

1 What decimal is shown on the hundredths square?

a. 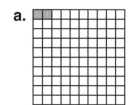   b. 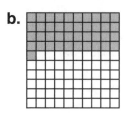   c. 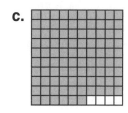   d.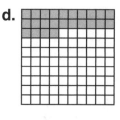

_____   _____   _____   _____

2 Color part of each hundredths square to match the given decimal.

a. 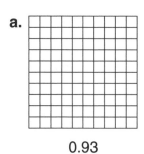   b. 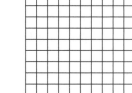   c. 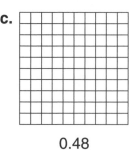   d.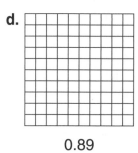

    0.93   0.16   0.48   0.89

3 Complete the chart for each decimal.

a. 0.73 | tenths | | hundredths | **b.** 0.11 | tenths | | hundredths |

c. 0.86 | tenths | | hundredths | **d.** 0.43 | tenths | | hundredths |

4 The decimal shown is _____.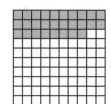

5 Color the hundredths square.   0.64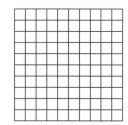

6 Complete the chart.   0.84 | tenths | | hundredths |

1 Write the decimal for each fraction.

a. $\frac{4}{10}$ _____

b. $\frac{6}{100}$ _____

c. $\frac{37}{100}$ _____

d. $\frac{61}{100}$ _____

2 Write the decimal for each mixed number.

a. $1\frac{1}{10}$ _____

b. $2\frac{7}{100}$ _____

c. $2\frac{71}{100}$ _____

d. $1\frac{33}{100}$ _____

3 Use a decimal to write each amount.

a. 2 tenths _____

b. 5 tenths _____

c. 2 hundredths _____

d. 59 hundredths _____

4 Write the decimal. $\frac{85}{100}$ _____

5 Write the decimal. $1\frac{3}{100}$ _____

6 Use a decimal to write *51 hundredths*. _____

Decimals and Fractions

1 Write the fraction.

    a. 6 tenths _____

    b. 9 tenths _____

    c. 81 hundredths _____

    d. 14 hundredths _____

2 Write the decimal.

    a. $\dfrac{3}{10}$ _____

    b. $\dfrac{4}{10}$ _____

    c. $\dfrac{23}{100}$ _____

    d. $\dfrac{74}{100}$ _____

3 Arrange in order from *least* to *greatest*.

    a. 0.2, 0.4, 0.3 _____

    b. 0.90, 0.61, 0.81 _____

    c. 1.6, 1.7, 1.2 _____

    d. 1.9, 2.2, 1.5 _____

4 Write the fraction for *58 hundredths*. _____

5 Write the decimal for $\dfrac{89}{100}$. _____

6 Arrange in order from *least* to *greatest*: 1.9, 2.7, 1.6 _____

1 Write *true* or *false* for each fraction statement.

  a. $\frac{1}{8} < \frac{3}{8}$ _____

  b. $\frac{1}{5} > \frac{2}{5}$ _____

  c. $\frac{1}{10} > \frac{5}{10}$ _____

  d. $\frac{3}{4} > \frac{1}{4}$ _____

2 Use the correct inequality sign, < or >, to make each fraction statement true.

  a. $\frac{1}{3} \square \frac{2}{3}$

  b. $\frac{3}{10} \square \frac{1}{10}$

  c. $\frac{2}{10} \square \frac{1}{10}$

  d. $\frac{1}{5} \square \frac{2}{5}$

3 Use the correct inequality sign, < or >, to make each decimal statement true.

  a. 0.5 $\square$ 0.9

  b. 0.3 $\square$ 0.1

  c. 0.7 $\square$ 1.0

  d. 0.25 $\square$ 0.75

4 Write *true* or *false*. $\frac{2}{10} < \frac{1}{10}$ _____

5 Use the correct inequality sign, < or >, to make the fraction statement true. $\frac{2}{3} \square \frac{1}{3}$

6 Use the correct inequality sign, < or >, to make the decimal statement true.   0.4 $\square$ 0.2

Decimal Addition

1 Add the decimals.

a.	Ones	Tenths
	0 .	2
+	0 .	3

b.	Ones	Tenths
	0 .	6
+	0 .	2

c.	Ones	Tenths
	0 .	1
+	0 .	2

d.	Ones	Tenths
	0 .	4
+	0 .	4

2 Add the decimals.

a.   1 . 5
   + 0 . 4

b.   3 . 2
   + 1 . 5

c.   1 . 4
   + 2 . 4

d.   1 . 6 3
   + 2 . 1 2

3   **a.** Add: 0.46 and 3.21 _____

    b. Find the sum: 1.86 and 2.11 _____

    c. Find the total: 9.03 and 0.46 _____

    d. Add: 1.48 and 2.51 _____

4 Add.

	Ones	Tenths
	0 .	3
+	0 .	5

5 Add.   1 . 2 6
   + 3 . 4 3

6 Find the sum: 1.63 and 2.16 _____

Decimal Subtraction

1 Subtract the decimals.

a.	Ones	Tenths
	0	6
−	0	2

b.	Ones	Tenths
	0	8
−	0	6

c.	Ones	Tenths
	0	9
−	0	8

d.	Ones	Tenths
	0	5
−	0	2

2 Subtract the decimals.

a. 1 . 8
     − 0 . 5

b. 6 . 9
     − 5 . 2

c. 9 . 4
     − 3 . 2

d. 8 . 6 4
     − 0 . 5 1

3 **a.** Subtract 1.63 from 2.98. _____

b. Find the difference between 3.59 and 2.46. _____

c. Find 4.36 minus 1.24. _____

d. Find 25.32 take away 14.11. _____

4 Subtract.

Ones	Tenths
0	8
− 0	7

5 Subtract.   4 . 9 3
               − 1 . 3 2

6 Find: 18.75 minus 12.32 _____

Decimal Addition and Subtraction with Regrouping

1 Add the decimals.

   a.   4 . 6
       + 2 . 9
      ―――――

   b.   4 . 2
       + 3 . 9
      ―――――

   c.   2 . 8
       + 4 . 6
      ―――――

   d.   6 . 3 5
       + 2 . 4 9
      ―――――

2 Subtract the decimals.

   a.   7 . 2
       − 4 . 4
      ―――――

   b.   8 . 5
       − 5 . 6
      ―――――

   c.   9 . 3
       − 3 . 9
      ―――――

   d.   7 . 3 4
       − 2 . 1 6
      ―――――

3 Find the . . .

a. total length of 1.55 yards and 2.35 yards. _____

b. difference between 0.85 yards and 0.59 yards. _____

c. sum of 1.63 gallons and 2.41 gallons. _____

d. change from $5.00 after spending $3.54. _____

4 Add.   2 . 7 3
          + 5 . 6 3
        ―――――

5 Subtract.   7 . 3 3
            − 2 . 1 5
          ―――――

6 Find the difference.   1.25 gallons and 0.71 gallons _____

Decimals Review

1 Order from *least* to *greatest*: 0.32, 0.40, 0.14, 0.03

_____   _____   _____   _____

2 Draw a line to match each decimal with the correct fraction.

$\frac{2}{10}$ $\frac{4}{10}$ $\frac{4}{100}$ $\frac{1}{10}$ 0.1   0.2   0.4   0.04

3 Write a decimal to represent the orange fish. There are 100 fish; 83 of the fish are orange.

_____

4 Order from *least* to *greatest* by first changing to all fractions or all decimals.

0.7 _____ $\frac{3}{10}$ _____   0.5 _____   0.2 _____ $\frac{9}{10}$ _____

_____   _____   _____   _____   _____

5 Circle the *greatest* number and box in the *least* number.   0.19   0.5   0.11   1.9

6 Now, write the numbers from question 5 in order from *least* to *greatest*.

_____   _____   _____   _____

7 Use the correct inequality sign, < or >, to make the statement true.   0.4 ☐ 0.2

8 Mr. Brown bought a sandwich for $1.55, a bottle of water for $1.80, and an apple for $0.80. How much did Mr. Brown spend on lunch? _____

9 Megan had $10.00 to spend. She bought a magazine for $5.75 and a chocolate bar for $1.20. How much change did Megan receive? _____

10 Find the difference of 1.25 and 0.71. _____

Simple Percentages

1 Look at the following signs. Answer the questions by writing the letter for the correct sign.

50% off	100% guaranteed	15% off storewide	20% free	5% new
A	**B**	**C**	**D**	**E**

a. Which is the greatest percentage? _____

b. Which is the least percentage? _____

c. Which percentage is the same as a half? _____

d. Which percentage is twenty percent? _____

2 Write each percent in numeral form.

a. ten percent _____   b. twenty-five percent _____

c. twelve percent _____   d. ninety-five percent _____

3 Write the correct inequality sign, < or >, in each box to complete each number sentence.

a. 20% ☐ 25%   b. 15% ☐ 10%

c. 90% ☐ 70%   d. 95% ☐ 30%

4 Look at the labels below. Which is the greatest percentage? _____

95% wheat	60% cream	5% pure juice
A	**B**	**C**

5 Write in numeral form: forty-five percent _____

6 Write the correct inequality sign, < or >, in the box to complete the number sentence.

50% ☐ 35%

Money – Coins

1 How many of each coin are needed to make $2?

    a. 50¢ coins _____   **b.** 25¢ coins _____   **c.** 5¢ coins _____   **d.** 10¢ coins _____

2 What is the least number of coins needed to make each amount? List the coins in the boxes below. Choose from $1, 50¢, 25¢, 10¢, 5¢, and 1¢ coins.

a. $1.45	**b.** $1.25	**c.** $1.95	**d.** $2.25

3 Six children each bought a toy ball that cost $2.25. They all used different sets of coins. Complete the grid to show the different combinations of coins they could have used.

		$1	50¢	25¢	10¢	5¢
a.	Jane					
b.	William					
c.	Yana					
d.	Violet					

4 How many 25¢ coins are needed to make $1? _____

5 What is the least number of coins needed to buy the cupcake? List the coins on the line. _____

$2.80

6 Peter and Robert each bought a pen for $2.95. Complete the grid to show the different coins they could have used.

		$1	50¢	25¢	10¢	5¢
a.	Peter					
b.	Robert					

Money – Bills

1 How many of each bill are needed to make $100?

a.

b.

c.

d.

_____   _____   _____   _____

2 What is the least number of bills that could be used to equal the amounts given? List the bills on the line. Choose from $100, $50, $20, $10, $5, $2, and $1 bills.

a. $75 _____   b. $93 _____

c. $108 _____   d. $169 _____

3 Find the total amount of money each person has and write it on the line.

a. Chris     _____

b. Jayne    _____

c. Julie      _____

4 How many  are needed to make $40? _____

5 What is the least number of bills needed to buy an item that costs $146? List the bills.

_____

6 Find the total amount of money Fiona has. _____

1 Add or subtract.

    a. $ 2 . 4 5
        + $ 1 . 3 5

    b. $ 3 . 4 5
        + $ 1 . 9 0

    c. $ 5 . 3 9
        – $ 0 . 9 8

    d. $ 6 . 9 0
        – $ 3 . 7 5

2 Find the total cost.

    a. a $1.95 sandwich and a $2.20 drink _____

    b. a $1.75 slice of pizza and a $2.40 drink _____

    c. a $2.25 salad and a 90¢ apple _____

    d. a $2.15 slice of cake and a $2.35 coffee _____

3 Find the change from . . .

    a. $5.00 after spending $3.00. _____

    b. $4.50 after spending $4.10. _____

    c. $10.00 after spending $8.30. _____

    d. $6.90 after spending $4.50. _____

4 Subtract. $ 9 . 2 5
            – $ 6 . 7 2

5 Find the total cost of a $2.95 fruit bar and a $2.30 orange juice. _____

6 Find the change from $2.00 after spending $0.65. _____

Money – Multiplication and Division

1 Multiply or divide.

a. $5.00 × 2 = _____

b. 5¢ × 3 = _____

c. $20.00 ÷ 10 _____

d. 90¢ ÷ 3 = _____

2 Find the total cost.

a. 3 apples at 20¢ each _____

b. 2 cans of dog food at $1.00 each _____

c. 5 chocolate candies at 10¢ each _____

d. 3 loaves of bread at $2.00 each _____

3 How many of each item could I buy for $10?

a. soda bottles at $2.00 each _____

b. golf balls at $1.00 each _____

c. sunscreen at $4.00 each _____

d. basketballs at $10.00 each _____

4 Multiply $5.00 × 3. _____

5 Find the total cost of 3 cartons of milk at $3.00 each. _____

6 How many oranges could I buy for $5.00 if each one cost $1.00? _____

Money – Rounding

1 Round each amount to the nearest dollar.

a. $6.05 _____   **b.** $5.95 _____   **c.** $9.75 _____

d. $3.15 _____   **e.** $10.98 _____   **f.** $18.89 _____

2 Round to the nearest 10 cents.

a. 92¢ _____   **b.** 57¢ _____   **c.** 26¢ _____

d. 43¢ _____   **e.** 89¢ _____   **f.** 64¢ _____

3 Round each amount to the nearest dollar and then add. The first one has been started for you.

a.	$ 4 . 6 5 ≈ $ 5 . 0 0 + $ 3 . 9 8 ≈ + _____ $ 9 . 0 0	**b.**	$ 7 . 3 5 + $ 4 . 6 7 + _____ _____
c.	$ 1 2 . 4 2 + $ 8 . 3 1 + _____ _____	**d.**	$ 8 . 9 7 + $ 6 . 6 5 + _____ _____

4 Round $8.95 to the nearest dollar. _____

5 Round 76¢ to the nearest 10 cents. _____

6 Round to the nearest dollar and then add.

$ 3 . 7 5 ⟶ $
+ $ 1 0 . 1 0 ⟶ + $

_____

Money – Estimating

1 Estimate each cost using the values given.

   a. $3 \times \$1.95$

      $\approx 3 \times \$2.00$

      $\approx$ _____

   c. $5 \times \$6.05$

      $\approx 5 \times$ _____

      $\approx$ _____

   b. $4 \times \$5.95$

      $\approx$ _____ $\times \$6.00$

      $\approx$ _____

   d. $9 \times \$2.98$

      $\approx 9 \times$ _____

      $\approx$ _____

2 Estimate each cost to the nearest dollar.

   a. $3 \times \$2.95 \approx$ _____

   c. $6 \times \$1.95 \approx$ _____

   b. $2 \times \$5.05 \approx$ _____

   d. $4 \times \$3.10 \approx$ _____

3 Estimate the change.

   a. $\$10.00 - \$7.98$

      $\approx \$10 - \$8$

      $\approx$ _____

   b. $\$10.00 - \$6.05$

      $\approx \$10 -$ _____

      $\approx$ _____

   c. $\$5.00 - \$3.95$

      $\approx \$5 -$ _____

      $\approx$ _____

   d. $\$5.00 - \$2.10$

      $\approx \$5 -$ _____

      $\approx$ _____

   e. $\$20.00 - \$16.80$

      $\approx$ _____ $-$ _____

      $\approx$ _____

   f. $\$20.00 - \$10.95$

      $\approx$ _____ $-$ _____

      $\approx$ _____

4 Estimate the cost by first rounding to the nearest dollar.

   $4 \times \$1.90 \approx 4 \times$ _____ $\approx$ _____

5 Estimate the total cost to the nearest dollar. $3 \times \$4.05 \approx$ _____

6 Estimate the change by first rounding to the nearest dollar.

   $\$10.00 - \$5.97 \approx \$10 -$ _____ $\approx$ _____

Symmetry

1 Use a pencil and a ruler to draw one line of symmetry on each picture.

a.   b.  c. 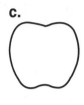 d.  e. 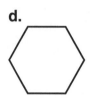 f.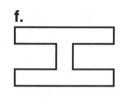

2 Which of the following shapes does not have a line of symmetry?

a.   b.   c.

d.   e.   f.

3 Complete each drawing so that it is symmetrical.

a.    b.   c.

4 Use a pencil and a ruler to draw a line of symmetry.

5 Does the shape  have a line of symmetry? _____

6 Complete the drawing so that it is symmetrical above and below the line.

Two-Dimensional Shapes

1 Circle the shape that does not belong.

a.  b.  c.

2

Which of the above shapes have . . .

a. 3 sides? _____   b. 4 sides? _____   c. all sides equal? _____

d. 6 sides? _____   e. 7 sides? _____   f. 5 sides? _____

3 How many corners does each of the following shapes have?

a.   b.   c.   d.   e.   f.

_____   _____   _____   _____   _____   _____

4 Match the name from the word list to the shape.

| circle | square | rectangle | rhombus | hexagon | triangle |

a. _____   b. _____   c. _____

d. _____   e. _____   f. _____

5 Circle the shape that does not belong.

6 Which shape does not have sides with equal lengths?

A   B   C   D   _____

7 How many corners does have? _____

Pentagons and Octagons

1 Count and record the number of sides and angles on each of the shapes.

a.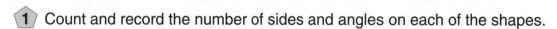

sides = _____

angles = _____

b.

sides = _____

angles = _____

c.

sides = _____

angles = _____

2 List the shapes below which are . . .

a. pentagons. _____

b. octagons. _____

3 How many sides are there on . . .

a. 2 pentagons? _____

b. 3 octagons? _____

c. 2 pentagons and 2 octagons? _____

d. 5 squares and 3 pentagons? _____

4 Count and record the number of sides and angles.

 sides = _____ angles = _____

5 List the shapes that are pentagons. _____

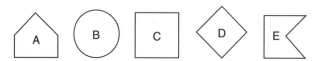

6 How many sides are there on 2 pentagons and 6 octagons? _____

Trapezoids and Parallelograms

1 Match the names with the shapes.

parallelogram	rectangle	oval	triangle	trapezoid	hexagon

a. _____

b. _____

c. _____

d. _____

e. _____

f. _____

2 Write the number of sides each of the shapes has.

a. square _____   **b.** rectangle _____   **c.** parallelogram _____   **d.** trapezoid _____

3 Circle the shapes that are trapezoids.

a.   b.   c.   d.   e.   f.

4 Circle the name of this shape.

parallelogram	octagon	rectangle	square

5 Which of the following shapes are trapezoids? _____

A   B   C   D

6 How many angles are there in 2 trapezoids and 4 parallelograms? _____

Shape Designs

1 Name the shapes.

a.

_____

b.

_____

c.

_____

d.

_____

e.

_____

f.

_____

2 Indicate the number of sides found on each of the shapes.

a.   b.   c.   d.   e.   f.

_____   _____   _____   _____   _____   _____

3 Circle the shapes that are rectangles.

a.   b.    c.   d.   e.   f.

4 Name the shape.   _____

5 Tell the number of sides found in the shape in number 4. _____

6 Draw a line inside the square to create 2 triangles.

1 Join the dots to complete the shape, and then state if it is *regular* or *irregular*.

a.   b.   c.   d.

_____   _____   _____   _____

2 Name these regular shapes.

a. △   b. □   c. ⬠

_____   _____   _____

d. ⯃   e. ⬡   f. ◇

_____   _____   _____

3 Name these irregular shapes.

a.   b.   c.

_____   _____   _____

d.   e.   f.

_____   _____   _____

4 Join the dots and state if the shape is *regular* or *irregular*.

_____

5 Name the *regular* shape. ▽ _____

6 Name the *irregular* shape. _____

Angles

1 For each of the following angles, indicate if they are *smaller* or *larger* than a right angle.

a. 　　　b. 　　　c. 　　　d.

_____　　　_____　　　_____　　　_____

2 For each of the following angles, indicate if they are *smaller* or *larger* than angle x.

a. 　　　b. 　　　c. 　　　d.

_____　　　_____　　　_____　　　_____

3 Order the following angles from the *smallest* (1) to the *largest* (6).

a. 　　b. 　　c. 　　d. 　　e. 　　f.

_____　_____　_____　_____　_____　_____

4 Is the angle *smaller* or *larger* than a right angle? _____

5 Is the angle 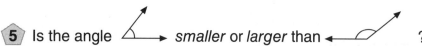 *smaller* or *larger* than  ? _____

6 Order the three angles from *smallest* (1) to *largest* (3).

_____　　　_____　　　_____

Right Angles

1 Circle the angles that are *smaller* than a right angle. Underline the angles that are *larger* than a right angle.

   a.    **b.** 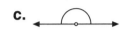 **c.**   **d.**   **e.**   **f.**

2 Circle the angles that are *right* angles.

   a.   **b.**    **c.**    **d.** 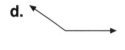   **e.** 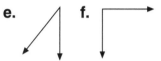 **f.**

3 Use the diagram to answer the questions.

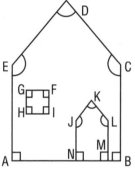

   a. Name 2 right angles. _____

   b. Name 2 angles larger than 90°. _____

   c. Name 2 angles smaller than 90°. _____

   d. Name 2 right angles on the window. _____

   e. Name 2 right angles on the door. _____

4 Is the angle  *smaller* or *larger* than a right angle? _____

5 Is the angle a *right* angle? _____

6 In the diagram, name 2 right angles. 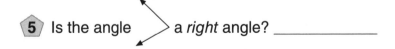 _____

Parallel Lines

1 Circle the sets of lines that show parallel lines.

a.   b.   c.   d.   e.   f.

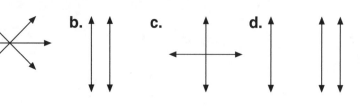

2 Indicate the parallel lines on each letter by tracing them.

a.   b.   c.   d.

3 Indicate the parallel lines on each shape by tracing each set in a different color. Some shapes will have more than one pair.

a.   b.   c.   d.

 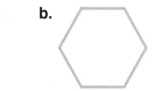  

4 Are the given lines parallel to each other?    _____

5 Indicate the parallel lines on the letter F by tracing them.

6 Does this shape contain parallel lines? _____

Perpendicular Lines

1 Circle the sets of lines that are perpendicular.

a.

b.

c.

d.

e.

f.

2 Trace the perpendicular lines on each shape.

a.

b.

c.

d.

3 Trace the perpendicular lines on each number. Some numbers may not have any perpendicular lines.

a.

b.

c.

d.

4 Are these lines perpendicular?  _____

5 Does the shape  show perpendicular lines? _____

6 Trace the perpendicular lines.

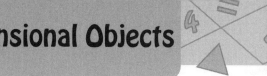

1 Name the shape of each shaded face.

a.   b.   c.   d.

_____   _____   _____   _____

2 Match each object with its name from the word list on the right.

a.   b.   c.

_____   _____   _____

d.   e.   f.

_____   _____   _____

cube

sphere

cylinder

cone

pyramid

triangular prism

3 How many surfaces does each object have?

a.   b.   c.    d.

_____   _____   _____   _____

4 Name the shape of the shaded face.

_____

5 Circle the name of the object shown in the picture.

cone   cylinder   rectangular prism

6 How many surfaces does the shape have? _____

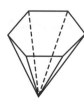

1 List the different shapes of the faces each solid contains.

a.

b.

_____ _____

_____ _____

c.

d.

_____ _____

_____ _____

2 Which of the following solids has . . .

A   B   C   D   E

a. 8 corners? _____

b. 5 faces? _____

c. 1 corner? _____

d. 12 edges? _____

e. 9 edges? _____

f. only curved surfaces? _____

3 What is the shape of the base for each of the following solids?

a.

b.

c.

d.

_____ _____ _____ _____

4 What shape are the faces of this solid?

  _____

5 Which of the following solids has only two flat surfaces? _____

A   B   C   D   E

Prisms and Cylinders

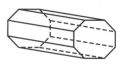

1 List the different shapes of the faces used in the construction of the three-dimensional shapes.

a. 　　　**b.** 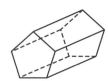　　　**c.**　　　**d.**

_____　　_____　　_____　　_____

_____　　_____　　_____　　_____

2 Label the item as a *cube*, *rectangular prism*, *cylinder*, or *sphere*.

a. 　　　**b.** 　　　**c.** 　　　**d.**

_____　　_____　　_____　　_____

3 How many faces does each of the following have?

a. 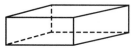　　　**b.**　　　**c.**　　　**d.**

_____　　_____　　_____

4 List the different shapes of the faces used in the shape below.

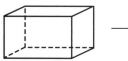　　_____

_____

5 Label 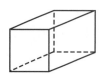 as *prism*, *cylinder*, or *neither*. _____

6 How many faces does have? _____

1 Which of the following are pyramids? _____

a.

b.

c.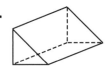

d.

e.

f.

2 How many faces does each of the following have?

a.

b.

c.

_____

_____

_____

d.

e.

f.

_____

_____

_____

3 Shade the base of each shape. Write the number of unshaded faces on the line next to the shape.

a. 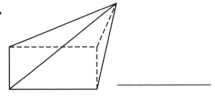 _____

b. 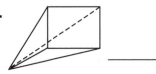 _____

c. _____

d. _____

4 Is 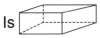 a pyramid? _____

5 How many faces does have? _____

1 How many faces (flat surfaces) does each solid have?

a. 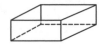   b.   c.   d.

_____   _____   _____   _____

2 Circle the two *nets* that would fold to make a cube.

a.   b.   c.   d.   e. 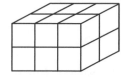   f.

3 How many blocks are used in the following constructions?

a. 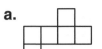   b.    c.   d.

_____   _____   _____   _____

4 How many faces does have? _____

5 Would the following *net* fold to make a cube? 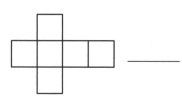 _____

6 How many blocks were used in the following construction? 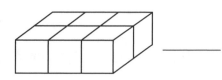 _____

Movement of Shapes

1 Use the word *reflection* (flip), *translation* (slide), or *rotation* (turn) to describe the movement of each shape.

a.

b.

c.

_____

_____

_____

d.

e.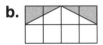

f.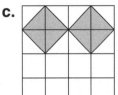

_____

_____

_____

2 Complete the patterns by *reflecting* (flipping) the tiles to the right or down.

a.

b.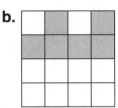

c.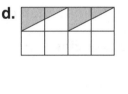

d.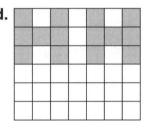

3 Complete the patterns by *translating* (sliding) tiles to the right and/or down.

a.

b.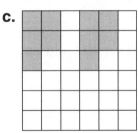

c.

d.

4 Use the word *reflection*, *translation*, or *rotation* to describe the picture below.

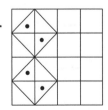 _____

5 Complete the pattern by *reflecting* tiles to the right.

6 Complete the pattern by *translating* the tiles to the right and down.

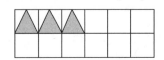

Position

1 Tell which item is . . .

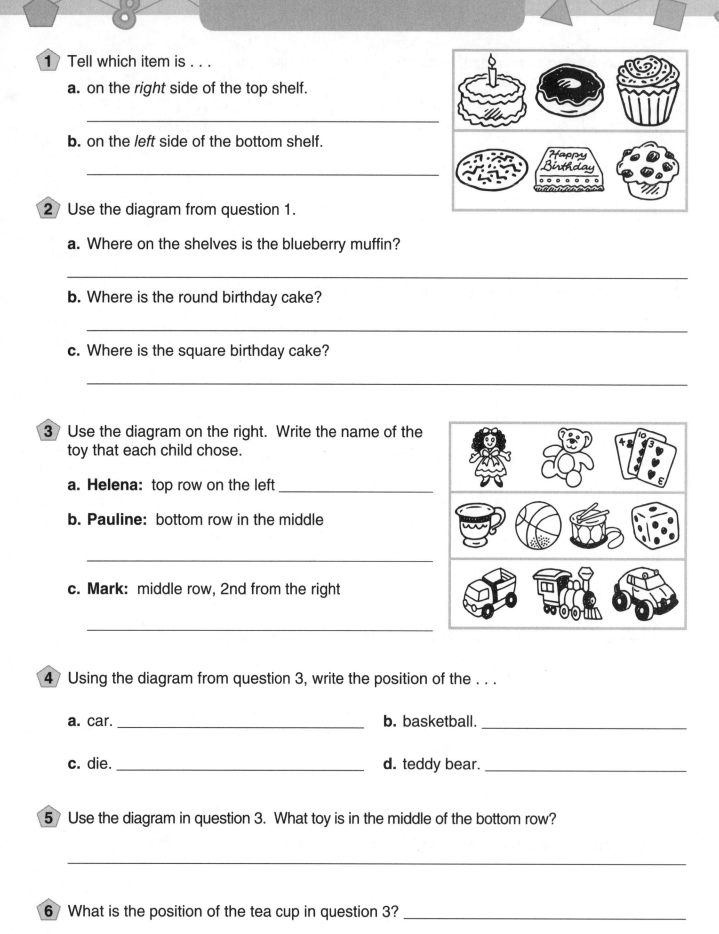

    a. on the *right* side of the top shelf.

    _____

    b. on the *left* side of the bottom shelf.

    _____

2 Use the diagram from question 1.

    a. Where on the shelves is the blueberry muffin?

_____

    b. Where is the round birthday cake?

_____

    c. Where is the square birthday cake?

_____

3 Use the diagram on the right. Write the name of the toy that each child chose.

    a. Helena: top row on the left _____

    b. Pauline: bottom row in the middle

    _____

    c. Mark: middle row, 2nd from the right

    _____

4 Using the diagram from question 3, write the position of the . . .

    a. car. _____
    b. basketball. _____

    c. die. _____
    d. teddy bear. _____

5 Use the diagram in question 3. What toy is in the middle of the bottom row?

_____

6 What is the position of the tea cup in question 3? _____

Compass Directions

1 What state is . . .

a. north of South Australia? _____

b. south of Victoria? _____

c. to the west of the Northern Territory? _____

d. to the north of New South Wales? _____

2 Which landmark is . . .

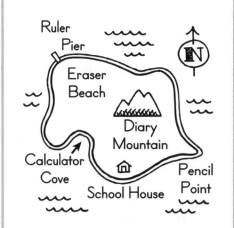

a. north of School House? _____

b. east of Diary Mountain? _____

c. southeast of Ruler Pier? _____

Give the direction of . . .

d. Eraser Beach from Diary Mountain. _____

e. Calculator Cove from School House. _____

f. Pencil Point from Diary Mountain. _____

3 Write the directions for Sam's boat to the . . .

a. shark. _____

b. dolphin. _____

c. island. _____

Where is Sam's boat from the . . .

d. turtle? _____

e. shark? _____

f. island? _____

4 On the map in question 1, what state is just to the south of New South Wales?

_____

5 On the map in question 2, what landmark is northwest of Calculator Cove?

_____

6 On the diagram in question 3, where is Sam's boat in relation to the dolphin?

_____

1 You are trying to reach the star at the end of the maze. Move the counter along the shaded path as directed and complete the answers in order.

a. move _____ right   **b.** move _____ up

c. move _____ left   **d.** move _____ up

e. move _____ left   **f.** move _____ down

g. To complete the path, move the counter _____ right.

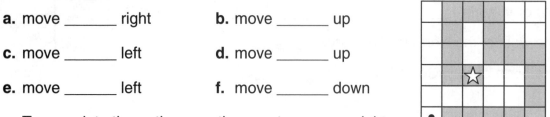

2 Follow the directions given to fill in the boxes to color the path of the mouse. Move . . .

     a. 7 right

     b. 5 up

     c. 6 left

     d. 3 down

     e. 4 right

     f. 1 up

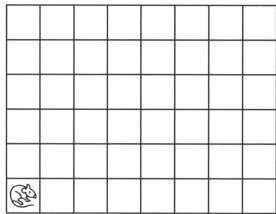

3 Add the direction *2 left* to complete the path in the diagram in question 2.

4 On the map, who lives on . . .

     a. Learn St.? _____

     b. House Rd.? _____

     c. Where is the shop? _____

     d. Who lives closest to the track? _____

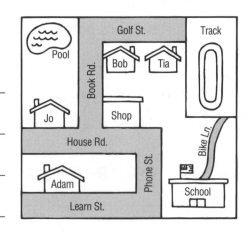

5 Using the map in question 4, describe the fastest way to go from the track to the school.

_____

_____

Coordinates

1 Follow the butterfly's path and give the letter at the point where it lands. (It begins at the start each time.)

   a. 3 up, 1 left, 3 right, and 3 up _____

   b. 3 up, 4 right, and 3 up _____

   c. 4 up, 2 right, and 2 up _____

   d. 3 up, 4 right, 2 down, 1 left, and 5 up _____

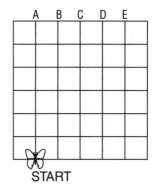

START

2 Use directions like those in question 1 to describe a path from . . .

   a. A to Y. _____

   b. B to Z. _____

   c. C to V. _____

   d. D to X. _____

3 Draw the symbol that is shown in the box with the given coordinates.

   a. A3 _____

   b. F5 _____

   c. B4 _____

   d. E2 _____

   e. C5 _____

   f. D5 _____

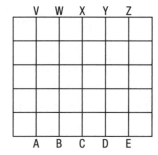

4 Using the grid from question 1, follow the butterfly's path and give the letter at the point where it lands if it goes 1 left, 4 up, 5 right, and 2 up. _____

5 Using the grid from question 2, give directions to describe a path from E to X.

_____

6 Using the grid from question 3, find the symbol at A4. _____

Digital and Analog Time

1 Read the times and write them on the digital clocks.

    a. 10 past 2   **b.** 25 past 5   **c.** 5 past 12   **d.** 8 past 8

2 Look at the clock faces and complete.

    a.    **b.**    **c.**    **d.**

    _____ past 9   _____ past 7   _____ past 1   _____ past 11

3 Draw the given times on each analog clock.

    a.    **b.**    **c.** 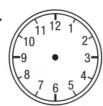   **d.**

    half past 11   quarter to 5   10 minutes past 10   7 o'clock

4 Read the time and write it on the digital clock.

                                       2 past 6

5 Look at the clock face and complete.

   _____ past 11

6 Draw *half past 2* on the analog clock.

Calendars

1 How many days are there in . . .

    a. one week? _____   **b.** two weeks? _____   **c.** January? _____

    d. September? _____   **e.** December? _____   **f.** June? _____

2 On which day of the week are the following dates?

    a. April 18 _____

    b. April 30 _____

    c. April 7 _____

    d. April 26 _____

April						
S	M	T	W	Th	F	S
					1	2
3	4	5	6	7	8	9
10	11	12	13	14	15	16
17	18	19	20	21	22	23
24	25	26	27	28	29	30

3 Use the December calendar and answer the questions.

    a. How many days are there in December? _____

    b. On what day of the week is December 1? _____

    c. Write the date of the last Thursday in December. _____

    d. How many Wednesdays are there in December? _____

December						
S	M	T	W	Th	F	S
				1	2	3
4	5	6	7	8	9	10
11	12	13	14	15	16	17
18	19	20	21	22	23	24
25	26	27	28	29	30	31

4 How many days are in November? _____

5 Looking at the month of April in question 2, on which day is April 20? _____

6 Looking at the month of December in question 3, on what day of the week does December

end? _____

Timelines and Timetables

1 Give the time you would arrive at the swimming pool . . .

    a. on the 9:00 train from Station Rd. _____

    b. on the 9:42 train from Short St. _____

    c. on the 10:15 train from Middle Plaza. _____

How long does it take the train to travel from . . .

    d. Station Rd. to the pool? _____

    e. Short Street to the pool? _____

    f. Station Rd. to Middle Plaza? _____

Train Timetable			
Station Rd.	9:00	9:30	10:00
Long Rd.	9:06	9:36	10:06
Short Street	9:12	9:42	10:12
Middle Plaza	9:15	9:45	10:15
Beral Lane	9:22	9:52	10:22
Round Rd.	9:27	9:57	10:27
Swimming Pool	9:30	10:00	10:30

2 Here is Veronica's morning schedule.

7:00	wake up
7:15	breakfast
7:30	get dressed
7:35	brush teeth
7:40	feed dogs
7:50	pack bag
8:00	leave for school
8:30	arrive at school
9:00	start school
10:15	morning break
10:45	end of break

a. What time is breakfast? _____

b. How many minutes does it take her to brush her teeth?

_____

c. How long does Veronica have to play at school before classes start?

_____

d. How long is the morning break? _____

3 Use the timetable from question 2 to fill in the timeline. The first activity is filled in.

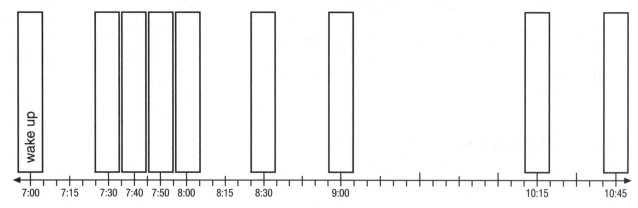

4 How long does it take for the train in question 1 to travel from Middle Plaza to the pool? _____

5 Using the information from question 2, at what time does morning break finish? _____

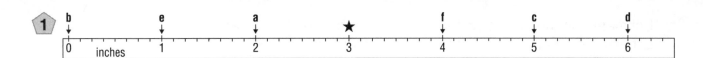

Length in Inches

1

| b | | e | | a | | ★ | | f | | c | | d |

0 inches 1 2 3 4 5 6

Give the length in inches to each letter above the ruler.

a. _____ in.   **b.** _____ in.   **c.** _____ in.

d. _____ in.   **e.** _____ in.   **f.** _____ in.

2 Measure the length to the point of each arrow.

a. _____

b.

_____

c. _____

d. _____

e. _____

f. _____

3 Use a ruler to draw lines having the given lengths.

a. 2 in.

b. 5 in.

c. 4 in.

d. 3 in.

4 Give the length in inches at the point marked with a star on the ruler in question 1. _____

5 Measure the length. _____

6 Use a ruler to draw a line 1 inch long in the box.

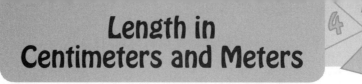

Length in Centimeters and Meters

1 Estimate and then measure the length of each side of the shapes in centimeters. Label the measurements in centimeters on the shapes.

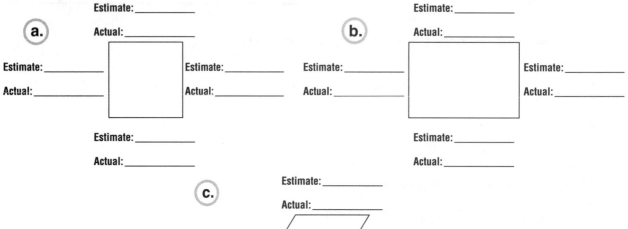

a.

Estimate: _____

Actual: _____

Estimate: _____

Actual: _____

Estimate: _____

Actual: _____

Estimate: _____

Actual: _____

b.

Estimate: _____

Actual: _____

Estimate: _____

Actual: _____

Estimate: _____

Actual: _____

Estimate: _____

Actual: _____

c.

Estimate: _____

Actual: _____

Estimate: _____

Actual: _____

Estimate: _____

Actual: _____

Estimate: _____

Actual: _____

2 Use the 1-cm dots to draw lines with the given lengths.

a. 5 cm • • • • • • • • • •

b. 7 cm • • • • • • • • • •

c. 3 cm • • • • • • • • • •

d. 1 cm • • • • • • • • • •

3 Would you use *meters* or *centimeters* to measure . . .

a. a pencil? _____   **b.** your hand? _____   **c.** a basketball court? _____

d. a tissue box? _____   **e.** your shoe? _____   **f.** your classroom? _____

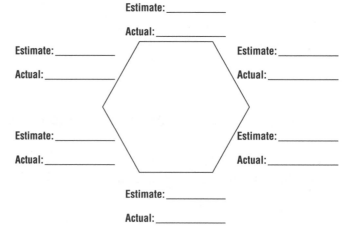

Estimate: _____

Actual: _____

Estimate: _____

Actual: _____

Estimate: _____

Actual: _____

4 Estimate and then measure the length of each side in centimeters.

Estimate: _____

Actual: _____

Estimate: _____

Actual: _____

Estimate: _____

Actual: _____

5 Use the 1-cm dots to draw a line 8 cm long. • • • • • • • • • •

6 Would you use meters or centimeters to measure the height of your desk? _____

1 Write these measurements in inches.

    a. 1 ft. 15 in. _____

    b. 1 ft. 82 in. _____

    c. 3 ft. 95 in. _____

    d. 2 ft. 11 in. _____

2 Write these measurements as feet and inches.

    a. 17 in. _____

    b. 33 in. _____

    c. 30 in. _____

    d. 16 in. _____

3 **Key**

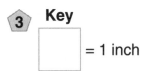

    ☐ = 1 inch

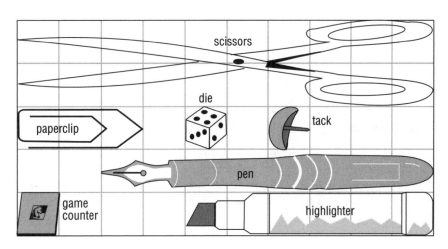

    a. Which object is the longest? _____

    b. Which objects are the same length? _____

    c. How long is the highlighter? _____

    d. The paper clip is _____ inches longer than the die.

4 Write *2 ft. 9 in.* in inches. _____

5 Write *65 in.* as feet and inches. _____

6 In the picture above, which object is 8 in. long? _____

Length in Millimeters

1 Write the given measurements in millimeters.

a. 1 cm 2 mm _____

b. 2 cm 8 mm _____

c. 3 cm 5 mm _____

d. 8 cm 3 mm _____

2 Write the given measurements as centimeters and millimeters.

a. 14 mm _____

b. 26 mm _____

c. 39 mm _____

d. 19 mm _____

3 Draw lines of these lengths using the 1-cm dots.

a. 50 mm   • • • • • • • • • •

b. 25 mm   • • • • • • • • • •

c. 10 mm   • • • • • • • • • •

d. 35 mm   • • • • • • • • • •

4 Write *2 cm 3 mm* in millimeters. _____

5 Write *52 mm* in centimeters and in millimeters. _____

6 Use the 1-cm dots to draw a line 30 mm long.

• • • • • • • • • •

Length with Decimals

1 Rewrite these measurements using meters and centimeters.

a. 1.23 m _____

b. 1.69 m _____

c. 3.72 m _____

d. 1.78 m _____

2 Use decimal form to write the measurements below.

a. 2 m 6 cm _____

b. 3 m 42 cm _____

c. 6 m 72 cm _____

d. 1 m 58 cm _____

3 Write these measurements using centimeters.

a. 27 mm _____

b. 2 m 40 cm _____

c. 49 mm _____

d. 1 m 25 cm _____

4 Rewrite *1.06 m* as meters and centimeters. _____

5 Use decimal form to write *3 m 75 cm*. _____

6 Write *1 m 19 cm* as centimeters. _____

Perimeter

1 Find the perimeter of each shape in inches. Write the answers in the shapes.

a.

b.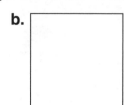

c.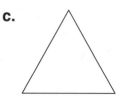

2 Find the perimeter of each shape. Use the measurements given.

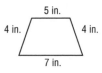 5 in. / 4 in. / 4 in. / 7 in.

  2 in. / 5 in. / 6 in.

  1 in. / 1 in. / 2 in. / 2 in.

1 in. / 2 in. / 1 in. / 3 in.

a. _____

b. _____

c. _____

d. _____

3 Draw each of the shapes described below. Show the measurements on each side.

a. a square with perimeter of 4 in.	**b.** a triangle with perimeter of 3 in.

c. a 4-sided shape with side lengths of 2 in., 2 in., 3 in., and 4 in.

4 Find the perimeter.   2 in. / 1 in. / 1 in. / 2 in.   The perimeter is _____

5 Draw a rectangle with perimeter of 8 inches on the back of this page.

Area

1 Find the area (in units) of each shape.

a.

b.

c.

_____ _____ _____

d.

e.

f.

_____ _____ _____

2 Rewrite each measurement using an abbreviation for the label.

a. three square yards _____   **b.** five square feet _____

c. nine square inches _____   **d.** sixteen square yards _____

3 Which unit of measurement, in.² or yd.², would you use to label the areas below?

a. a tennis court _____   **b.** the top of a matchbox _____

c. a kitchen floor _____   **d.** a CD cover _____

4 Find the area.

5 Use an abbreviation to write *twenty square feet*. _____

6 Which unit of measurement, in.² or yd.², would you use to find the area of the top of a

swimming pool? _____

Capacity in Liters

1

A   B   C   D   E

a. Which container would hold the *most* water? _____

b. Which container would hold the *least* water? _____

c. Which container would hold *more* water than C but less than B? _____

d. Which containers would hold *more* water than E? _____

2 Circle the objects that would hold *more* than one liter.

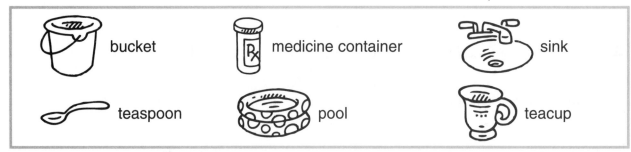

bucket   medicine container   sink

teaspoon   pool   teacup

3 5 L juice   2 L milk

A   B

a. What is the capacity of A? _____   **b.** What is the capacity of B? _____

c. Which container holds *more*? _____   **d.** How much more does it hold? _____

4 Which of the containers holds *more* than 5 L? _____   

A   B   C

5 Does a swimming pool hold *more* than one liter? _____

6 What is the capacity of container A?

_____

A   B

2 L orange juice   3 L milk

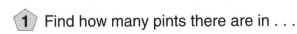

Capacity – Formal

1 Find how many pints there are in . . .

    a. 1 gallon _____   **b.** 2 quarts _____

    c. 3 gallons _____   **d.** 5 gallons _____

2 These containers measure pints. Use the numbers in each container to answer the questions.

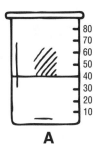 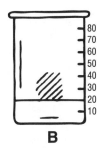 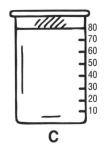 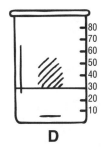

        A   B   C   D

    a. How much water is in container **C**? _____

    b. How much water is in container **D**? _____

    c. How much *more* water would be in container **A** than **B**? _____

    d. How much *more* water would be in container **A** than **D**? _____

3 Circle the objects that would hold *less than* one gallon when full.

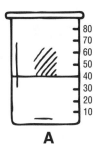 a cereal bowl   a swimming pool   a small jam jar

 a bathtub   a medicine dropper   a trough

4 How many *pints* are there in 9 gallons? _____

5 How many *gallons* of water would be in this container? _____

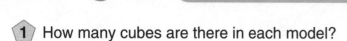
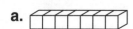
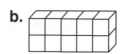

1 How many cubes are there in each model?

a.

_____ cubes

b.

_____ cubes

c.

_____ cubes

d.

_____ cubes

2 Write each measurement using an abbreviation for the units.

a. 3 cubic inches _____

b. 25 cubic feet _____

c. 13 cubic yards _____

d. 1 cubic inch _____

3 What is the volume of each model if each cube is 1 in.³?

a.

_____

b.

_____

c.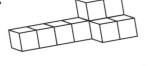

_____

d.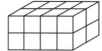

_____

4 How many cubes are there?   _____

5 Use the abbreviation to write *17 cubic inches*. _____

6 What is the volume if each cube is 1 in.³? _____

Cubic Centimeters

1 Find the volume by counting the number of centimeter cubes used in each construction.

a.

_____

b.

_____

c.

_____

d.

_____

2 Of the constructions in question 1 . . .

a. which object has the *largest* volume? _____

b. which object has the *smallest* volume? _____

c. which two objects have the *same* volume? _____

d. which object has a volume of *more* than 7 cm³? _____

3 If the following objects are made from cubes, find the volumes. Label volumes as *units³*.

	Length	Width	Height	Volume
a.	4	1	1	
b.	3	1	2	
c.	2	2	2	
d.	3	2	3	

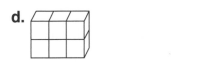

4 Find the volume by counting the number of centimeter cubes used in the construction.

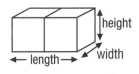

_____

5 Of the constructions in question 1, which object has a volume of 4 cm³? _____

6 Find the volume of an object that has a length of 1 cube, a width of 2 cubes, and a height of 5 cubes. _____

Arrangements

1 How many different ways can you arrange each of the following in a row?

a.  ☐△◯

b. 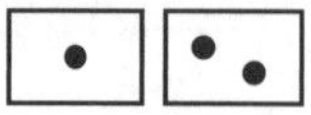 [•] [••]

c.  ☆☆☾

d.  ◯◁◯◠

_____   _____   _____   _____

2 4 pink doughnuts, 2 brown doughnuts, and 3 yellow doughnuts are placed in a bag. Which color is . . .

a. *most* likely to be selected first? _____

b. *least* likely to be selected first? _____

c. *most* likely to be selected last? _____

d. If a pink doughnut is selected, could the next one selected be . . .

pink? _____   yellow? _____   green? _____

3 The menu at a school cafeteria is shown below.

a. How many different lunches are there? _____

b. How many different drinks are there? _____

c. Scarlett had a salad. How many different drinks could she have with it? _____

d. If Emily had pizza but wanted another different lunch item, how many did she have to select from?

_____

Lunch	Drinks
salad	orange juice
pizza	milk
hot dog	water
sandwich	

4 How many different ways can you arrange 😊 😦 😮 in a row? _____

5 There are 5 circles, 4 squares, and 8 triangles in a bag. If one shape is selected at random, which shape is *most* likely to be chosen? _____

6 Use the menu in question 3 to answer. Adam did not like water. How many other drinks did he have to select from? _____

Chance

1 Look at the spinner.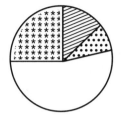

   a. How many different outcomes are possible? _____

   b. Do all outcomes have the same chance of occuring? _____

   c. Which outcome is the *most* likely? _____

   d. Which outcome is the *least* likely? _____

2 For the spinner, answer *true* or *false*.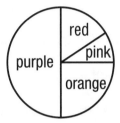

   a. Orange is the *most* likely color to be spun. _____

   b. Pink is the *least* likely color to be spun. _____

   c. There is no chance of spinning yellow. _____

   d. It is *more* likely to spin red than orange. _____

3 For the spinner, color according to the following statements.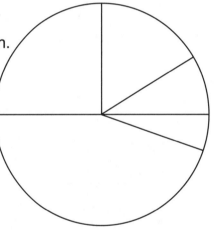

   a. The area that has the *least* chance of being spun is green.

   b. The area that has the *greatest* chance of being spun, fill with stars.

   c. There are dots in the area that is the 2nd *most* likely to be spun.

   d. The area that is the 2nd *least* likely to be spun has triangles.

   e. There are stripes in the remaining area.

4 For the spinner in question 1, are the stripes *more* likely to be spun than the dots? _____

5 For the spinner in question 2, answer *true* or *false*.

   There is an equal chance of spinning either orange *or* red and pink together. _____

6 Color the area of the spinner . . .

   • which has the *least* chance, blue.

   • which has the *greatest* chance, yellow.

   • which has a *greater* chance than blue, but *less* chance than yellow, of being spun green.

Picture Graphs

1 The number of toys sold is shown on the graph.

Toys Sold	 = 1
Monday	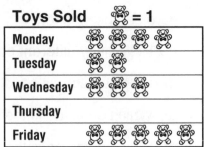
Tuesday	
Wednesday	
Thursday	
Friday	

a. How many toys were sold on Wednesday? _____

b. On which day were the *most* toys sold? _____

c. On which day were the *least* toys sold? _____

d. How many *more* toys were sold on Monday than Tuesday? _____

2 This is a graph of the students' favorite fruits.

Students' Favorite Fruits

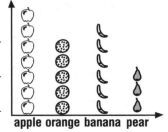

apple orange banana pear

(each piece of fruit = 1 student)

a. What is the *most* popular fruit? _____

b. What is the *least* popular fruit? _____

c. How many students liked oranges the best? _____

d. How many *more* students liked apples than oranges? _____

3 Albert collected information about different-colored eyes. Use the information to create a picture graph.

Students' Eye Colors

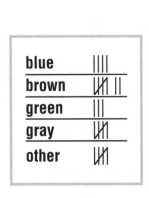

blue					
brown	𝗟𝗛𝗟		
green				
gray	𝗟𝗛𝗟
other	𝗟𝗛𝗟

Number of People

blue   brown   green   gray   other

Color

Key: 👁 = 1 person

4 Using the information from question 1, what was the total number of toys sold on Monday and Friday? _____

5 In question 2, what was the total number of students asked about their favorite fruit? _____

6 Using the information from question 3, what was the most common eye color? _____

Reading Tables

1 Meryl sorted all of the pencils into different-colored groups and recorded the information in a table.

Red	Blue	Green	Yellow	Brown	Pink	Black
3	6	5	9	15	12	4

a. What was the *most* common color? _____

b. What was the *least* common color? _____

c. Which color is there 3 times more of than green? _____

d. What is the total number of black and brown pencils? _____

2 Here is a table showing the number of stamps and coins collected by a group of children.

	Stamps	Coins
Alfred	29	36
Betty	32	19
Conrad	50	25
David	16	48
Erin	45	27

How many stamps have been collected by . . .

a. Alfred? _____   **b.** David? _____   **c.** Erin? _____

How many coins have been collected by . . .

d. Betty? _____   **e.** Conrad? _____   **f.** Erin? _____

3 Here is some information about insects collected in the backyard. Use the information to complete the following table.

| | ants | bees | flies | butterflies |

Insects	Tally	Number
ants		
bees		
flies		
butterflies		

4 Use the information from question 1. What was the total number of pencils? _____

5 What was the total number of items Betty collected in question 2? _____

6 Use the information from question 3. What was the total number of insects found? _____

Bar Graphs

1 Interpret the following graph about different foods.

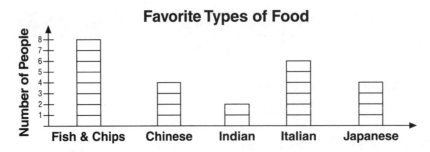

Favorite Types of Food

a. What foods have the same popularity? _____

b. How many more people like Italian than Japanese? _____

c. How many more people like Italian than Indian? _____

d. How many people liked the two most popular foods? _____

2 Simone surveyed a parking lot with different-colored cars. The boxes below represent the cars and are marked with the first letters of the colors. Complete the following tally sheet.

W	R	R	W	W	G	Y	Y	B	Y
G	W	Y	B	W	G	R	W	W	P
R	W	W	R	Y	R	R	R	B	B

Color	white	red	yellow	green	blue	pink
Tally						

3 From the tally sheet in question 2, create a bar graph.

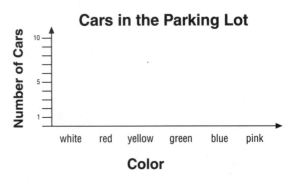

Cars in the Parking Lot

4 Go back to the graph in question 1. How many people were asked about their favorite foods?

_____

5 Three more cars pulled into the parking lot and they were all pink. Add them to your tally in question 2 and your bar graph in question 3 in a different color.

6 If there were 40 parking spaces in the parking lot, how many are now empty? _____

Guided Problem Solving

1 There are 25 parrots in 1 cage and 49 canaries in another. How many birds all together?

    a. What is the question asking you to find? _____

    b. How many parrots? _____

    c. How many canaries? _____

    d. Name the operation that needs to be used to solve. _____

    e. Write a number sentence. _____

    f. Write the answer. _____

2 Greg planted flowers in rows of 7. He planted 8 full rows and had 6 flowers left. How many plants were there all together?

    a. What is the question asking you to find? _____

    b. How many rows were there? _____

    c. How many plants were there in each row? _____

    d. How many plants were left over? _____

    e. Name the operations that need to be used. _____

    f. Find the answer. _____

3 How many rows of blocks could you make if you had 48 blocks and put 6 in each row?

    a. What is the question asking you to find? _____

    b. How many blocks in total? _____

    c. How many blocks in each row? _____

    d. Name the operation that needs to be used. _____

    e. Write a number sentence. _____

    f. Write the answer. _____

4 There were 20 books in the cupboard, and the teacher added another 13. What operation would be used to find the total number of books? _____

5 There are 6 cans in a package, and the box has 9 packages. What operation would be used to find the total number of cans? _____

6 Six workers shared 24 cookies equally. How would you find the number of cookies each worker received? _____

Problem Solving

1 **a.** The zoo has 9 lions and 17 tigers. How many big cats are there all together? _____

b. There are 59 public drinking fountains at the zoo and 12 for the staff. How many drinking fountains are there all together? _____

c. On Monday there were 32 frogs, and on Friday there were 67 frogs in total. How many frogs had been added during the week? _____

d. On Wednesday there were 19 chicks and by Thursday there were 26 chicks. How many chicks had hatched overnight? _____

2 How many were there all together?

a. There were 5 cows in each of 6 corrals. _____

b. There were 4 sheep in each of 7 corrals. _____

How many are there in each pen?

c. 10 chickens to be placed evenly in 2 pens. _____

d. 18 ducks to be placed evenly in 3 pens. _____

3 **a.** If I have $5.00, $16.25, and $14.30, how much money do I have in total? _____

b. If I had $100 and spent $8, how much is left? _____

c. I have five $5 bills and six $2 bills. I have _____ all together.

d. If $15.00 had to be divided evenly between 3 people, how much would each person receive? _____

4 The zoo has 68 keepers and 25 office staff. How many employees are there all together? _____

5 There were 5 rabbits in each of 4 cages. How many rabbits were there all together? _____

6 I bought a magazine for $5.90. If I paid $7.00, how much change did I receive? _____

Answer Key

Page 6
1. **a.** 205   **b.** 326   **c.** 767
2. **a.** 297   **b.** 801   **c.** 49
3. **a.** two hundred twenty-six
   b. fifty-six
   c. one hundred two
4. **a.** 162   **b.** 902
5. 415
6. 983
7. six hundred twenty-one
8. 316

Page 7
1. **a.** 123   **b.** 406
2. **a.** 5 or 5 ones   **b.** 500 or 5 hundreds   **c.** 50 or 5 tens
3. **a.** 306   **b.** 111   **c.** 272
4. **a.** 780   **b.** 290
5. 50 or 5 tens
6. 251

Page 8
1. **a.** 1,269   **b.** 2,618   **c.** 9,346   **d.** 8,982
2. **a.** 2,680   **b.** 6,706
3. **a.** six thousand three hundred eight
   b. five thousand two hundred fifty-one
   c. one thousand six
4. **a.** 5,021   **b.** 6,204
5. 3,049
6. two thousand three hundred forty-six

Page 9
1. **a.** 2   **b.** 1   **c.** none
2. **a.** true   **b.** false   **c.** false
   d. true   **e.** true   **f.** false
3. **a.** 206, 210, 220, 236   **b.** 678, 687, 786, 876
4. **a.** 603, 301, 205, 103   **b.** 132, 125, 119, 108
5. 0
6. **a.** true   **b.** false   **c.** true
7. 198, 208, 298, 691
8. 896, 696, 526, 325

Page 10
1. **a.** 64   **b.** 116   **c.** 57   **d.** 108
2. **a.** 40, 50, 60   **b.** 130, 140, 150
   c. 102, 122   **d.** 423, 433
3. **a.** 70, 60, 50   **b.** 470, 460, 450
   c. 47, 37, 27   **d.** 285, 255
4. 59
5. 86, 96, 106
6. 92, 82, 72

Page 11
1. **a.** 300; 500   **b.** 450; 650   **c.** 821; 1,021
   d. 663; 863   **e.** 1,130; 1,330   **f.** 1,469; 1,669
2. **a.** 400, 500, 600   **b.** 398, 498, 598
   c. 751, 851, 951   **d.** 1,050; 1,150; 1,250
3. **a.** 600, 500, 400   **b.** 501, 401, 301
   c. 260, 160, 60   **d.** 499, 399, 299
4. **a.** 765; 965   **b.** 99; 299
5. 1,785; 1,885
6. 463, 363, 263

Page 12
1. **a.** 28   **b.** 33   **c.** 34
   d. 36   **e.** 31   **f.** 30
2. **a.** 34   **b.** 30   **c.** 32
   d. 28   **e.** 36   **f.** 19
3. **a.** 57   **b.** 62   **c.** 59
   d. 57   **e.** 64   **f.** 54
4. 42
5. 18
6. 30

Page 13
1. **a.** ▲ ■ ▲   **b.** ▲ ▼ ▲
   c.    **d.**
2. **a.** 8, 10, 12   **b.** 32, 40, 48   **c.** 7, 9, 11
   d. 25, 30, 35   **e.** 15, 18, 21   **f.** 27, 29, 31
3. **a.** add 4   **b.** divide by 2   **c.** multiply by 2
4.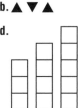
5. 22, 26, 30
6. add 3

Page 14
1. **a.** | 2 | H | 2 | T | 6 | 0 | **b.** | 4 | H | 0 | T | 9 | 0 |
   c. | 6 | H | 7 | T | 0 | 0 | **d.** | 1 | H | 1 | T | 1 | 0 |
   e. | 0 | H | 8 | T | 0 | 0 | **f.** | 8 | H | 0 | T | 2 | 0 |
2. **a.** 625   **b.** 269   **c.** 307
   d. 836   **e.** 480   **f.** 999
3. **a.** 600 or 6 hundreds   **b.** 90 or 9 tens
   c. 1 or 1 one   **d.** 50 or 5 tens
   e. 100 or 1 hundred   **f.** 0 or 0 ones
4. | 5 | H | 0 | T | 7 | 0 |

Page 14 *(cont.)*

5. 703

6. 5 or 5 ones

Page 15

1. a. 1,623   **b.** 4,387   **c.** 2,405   **d.** 8,042

2. a. | 6 | Th | 2 | H | 4 | T | 1 | O | **b.** | 7 | Th | 7 | H | 7 | T | 7 | O |

   c. | 2 | Th | 0 | H | 4 | T | 9 | O | **d.** | 1 | Th | 4 | H | 0 | T | 6 | O |

3. a. 2,000 or 2 thousands   **b.** 60 or 6 tens

   c. 10 or 1 ten   **d.** 300 or 3 hundreds

   e. 6,000 or 6 thousands   **f.** 800 or 8 hundreds

4. 3,702

5. | 5 | Th | 2 | H | 7 | T | 5 | O |

6. 300 or 3 hundreds

Page 16

1. a. | 4 | Th | 5 | H | 2 | T | 6 | O | **b.** | 6 | Th | 0 | H | 4 | T | 9 | O |

   c. | 8 | Th | 4 | H | 0 | T | 7 | O | **d.** | 9 | Th | 2 | H | 6 | T | 0 | O |

2. a. 2,578; 7,582; 8,572; 8,752   **b.** 1,999; 2,500; 2,870; 3,420

   c. 249; 870; 972; 1,672   **d.** 1,098; 1,111; 2,671; 4,213

3. a. 9,421   **b.** 8,763   **c.** 8,432

   d. 6,642   **e.** 9,210   **f.** 4,321

4. | 2 | Th | 3 | H | 1 | T | 0 | O |

5. 909; 1,021; 1,051; 1,161; 1,211

6. 9,831

Page 17

1. a. >   **b.** >   **c.** <

   d. <   **e.** >   **f.** >

2. a. true   **b.** false   **c.** true

   d. true   **e.** false   **f.** false

3. a. <   **b.** <   **c.** >

   d. >   **e.** <   **f.** <

4. >

5. true

6. <

Page 18

1. a. 13   **b.** 15   **c.** 16

   d. 12   **e.** 16   **f.** 13

2. a. 23   **b.** 17   **c.** 22

   d. 29   **e.** 23   **f.** 18

3. a. 16   **b.** 17   **c.** 12

4. 19

5. 26

6. 18

Page 19

1. a. 40; 33   **b.** 70; 63   **c.** 90; 91   **d.** 60; 54

2. a. 57   **b.** 73   **c.** 6; 63   **d.** 5; 63

3. a. 86   **b.** 53   **c.** 71

   d. 93   **e.** 64   **f.** 93

4. 100; 93

5. 30; 7; 93

6. 72

Page 20

1. a. 76   **b.** 83   **c.** 81   **d.** 73

2. a. 81 eggs

   b. 57 fish

   c. 71 candies

3. a. 15

4	9	2
3	5	7
8	1	6

b. 33

14	9	10
7	11	15
12	13	8

c. 36

11	16	9
10	12	14
15	8	13

d. 21

6	11	4
5	7	9
10	3	8

4. 58

5. $64

6. 66

28	18	20
14	22	30
24	26	16

Page 21

1. a. 914   **b.** 872   **c.** 932   **d.** 985

2. a. 631   **b.** 873   **c.** 431   **d.** 636

3. a. $478   **b.** $420   **c.** $943   **d.** $674

4. 584

5. 734

6. $445

Page 22

1. a. 900   **b.** 1,100   **c.** 1,700

   d. 1,100   **e.** 1,400   **f.** 1,400

2. a. 37 + 6 = 37 + 3 + 3   **b.** 28 + 8 = 28 + 2 + 6
     = 40 + 3   = 30 + 6
     = 43   = 36

   c. 42 + 9 = 42 + 8 + 1   **d.** 38 + 5 = 38 + 2 + 3
     = 50 + 1   = 40 + 3
     = 51   = 43

   e. 29 + 7 = 29 + 1 + 6   **f.** 64 + 7 = 64 + 6 + 1
     = 30 + 6   = 70 + 1
     = 36   = 71

3. a. 14   **b.** 26   **c.** 23

   d. 28   **e.** 27   **f.** 26

4. 900

5. 28

6. 35

Page 23

1. $14

2. 19

3. 14

4. Check sums for accuracy.

5. 28 people

6. 3; 5

7. 62 animals

8. Check sums for accuracy.

9. hat and book; game and radio; hat, CD, and calculator

Page 24

1. **a.** 200 **b.** 300 **c.** 500
   d. 200 **e.** 500 **f.** 400

2. **a.** 170 **b.** 430 **c.** 860
   d. 410 **e.** 400 **f.** 210

3. **a.**
$$\begin{array}{r} 31 + 63 \\ \approx\ 30 + 60 \\ \hline \approx\ \ \ \ 90 \end{array}$$
   b.
$$\begin{array}{r} 39 + 41 \\ \approx\ 40 + 40 \\ \hline \approx\ \ \ \ 80 \end{array}$$
   c.
$$\begin{array}{r} 81 + 22 \\ \approx\ 80 + 20 \\ \hline \approx\ \ \ 100 \end{array}$$
   d.
$$\begin{array}{r} 59 - 22 \\ \approx\ 60 - 20 \\ \hline \approx\ \ \ \ 40 \end{array}$$
   e.
$$\begin{array}{r} 87 - 31 \\ \approx\ 90 - 30 \\ \hline \approx\ \ \ \ 60 \end{array}$$
   f.
$$\begin{array}{r} 71 - 28 \\ \approx\ 70 - 30 \\ \hline \approx\ \ \ \ 40 \end{array}$$

4. 500

5. 820

6. **a.** 90
   b. 50

Page 25

1. **a.**
   $9 + 6 + 15 + 20$
   Estimate: $10 + 10 + 20 + 20 \approx 20$ or 60 or 100
   b.
   $15 + 20 + 25 + 30$
   Estimate: $20 + 20 + 30 + 30 \approx 10$ or 50 or 100

2. **a.**
   $30 + 60 + 50 + 21$
   Estimate: $30 + 60 + 50 + 20 \approx 130$ or 160 or 190
   b.
   $46 + 24 + 59 + 63$
   Estimate: $50 + 20 + 60 + 60 \approx 150$ or 190 or 230

3. **a.**
   $90 - 1 - 1 - 1 - 1$
   Estimate: $90 - 0 - 0 - 0 - 0 \approx 90$ or 70 or 50
   b.
   $140 - 8 - 6 - 5 - 2 - 7$
   Estimate: $140 - 10 - 10 - 10 - 0 - 10 \approx 120$ or 90 or 100

4. 50

5. 170

6. 90

Page 26

1. **a.** 4 **b.** 12 **c.** 10
   d. 2 **e.** 11 **f.** 2

2. **a.** 5 **b.** 8 **c.** 6
   d. 12 **e.** 9 **f.** 4

3. **a.** $6 - 2 = 4$ **b.** $10 - 4 = 6$ **c.** $12 - 5 = 7$
   d. $12 - 7 = 5$ **e.** $11 - 5 = 6$ **f.** $6 - 6 = 0$

4. 10

5. 6

6. $16 - 6 = 10$

Page 27

1. **a.** 5; 50; 500 **b.** 7; 70; 700
   c. 4; 40; 400 **d.** 2; 20; 200

2. **a.** $13 - 10 = 3$ **b.** $14 - 10 = 4$ **c.** $15 - 10 = 5$

3. **a.** 3; 8 **b.** 12; 8 **c.** 14; 5 **d.** 9; 6

4. 7; 70; 700

5. 9

6. 8; 7

Page 28

1. **a.** $30 - 12$: **think**
$$\begin{array}{r} 30 - 10 - 2 \\ = \ \ 20\ \ - 2 \\ = \ \ 18 \end{array}$$
   b. $24 - 11$: **think**
$$\begin{array}{r} 24 - 10 - 1 \\ = \ \ 14\ \ - 1 \\ = \ \ 13 \end{array}$$
   c. $46 - 13$: **think**
$$\begin{array}{r} 46 - 10 - 3 \\ = \ \ 36\ \ - 3 \\ = \ \ 33 \end{array}$$
   d. $47 - 22$: **think**
$$\begin{array}{r} 47 - 20 - 2 \\ = \ \ 27\ \ - 2 \\ = \ \ 25 \end{array}$$
   e. $39 - 12$: **think**
$$\begin{array}{r} 39 - 10 - 2 \\ = \ \ 29\ \ - 2 \\ = \ \ 27 \end{array}$$
   f. $36 - 23$: **think**
$$\begin{array}{r} 36 - 20 - 3 \\ = \ \ 16\ \ - 3 \\ = \ \ 13 \end{array}$$

2. **a.** 32 **b.** 34 **c.** 12 **d.** 15

3. **a.** 15 **b.** 42 **c.** 11 **d.** 22

4. 20; 8; 21

5. 32

6. 42

Page 29

1. **a.** 81 **b.** 42 **c.** 22 **d.** 42

2. **a.** 6 **b.** 7 **c.** 2 **d.** 7

3. **a.** 31 **b.** 41 **c.** 25 **d.** 25

4. 61

5. 52

6. 26

Page 30

1. **a.** 16 **b.** 33 **c.** 63 **d.** 44

2. **a.** 58 **b.** 28 **c.** 15 **d.** 58

3. **a.** 28; 28 **b.** 37; 37
   c. 17; 17; 92 **d.** 46; 46; 75

4. 44

5. 27

6. 27; 27; 91

Page 31

1. **a.**
$$\begin{array}{r} 9\ 3\ 5 \\ -\ 7\ 2\ 2 \\ \hline 2\ 1\ 3 \end{array}$$
   b.
$$\begin{array}{r} 4\ 9\ 9 \\ -\ 3\ 4\ 3 \\ \hline 1\ 5\ 6 \end{array}$$
   c.
$$\begin{array}{r} 7\ 5\ 6 \\ -\ 5\ 4\ 5 \\ \hline 2\ 1\ 1 \end{array}$$
   d.
$$\begin{array}{r} 8\ 9\ 6 \\ -\ 6\ 4\ 3 \\ \hline 2\ 5\ 3 \end{array}$$

2. **a.** $184 **b.** $12 **c.** $50 **d.** $134

3. **a.** $81 **b.** $60 **c.** $73

4.
$$\begin{array}{r} 3\ 9\ 8 \\ -\ 2\ 4\ 2 \\ \hline 1\ 5\ 6 \end{array}$$

5. $154

6. $176

Page 32

1. **a.** 12 **b.** 7 **c.** 27
   d. 66 **e.** 75 **f.** 85
2. **a.** $0.15 **b.** 6 **c.** 18 **d.** 16
3. **a.** 18; 28 **b.** 7; 17; 6 **c.** 6; 21; 5
   d. 5; 7; 32 **e.** 5; 24; 25 **f.** 7; 19; 36
4. 23
5. 9
6. 8; 9; 37

Page 33

1. **a.**

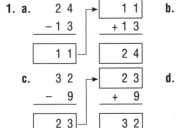

   c.

2. **a.** 23; 23 + 36 = 59 **b.** 23; 23 + 51 = 74
   c. 9; 9 + 37 = 46 **d.** 27; 27 + 25 = 52
3. **a.** correct **b.** 41 miles **c.** 33 miles **d.** correct
4.

5. 24; 24 + 17 = 41
6. yes

Page 34

1.

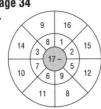

2. $9
3. 33
4. **a.** 37 − 6 does not equal 43. **b.** 31 marbles
5. $4
6. Check differences for accuracy.
7. $22
8. 20 − 9 = 11; 20 − 11 = 9
9. 874
10. Check differences for accuracy.

Page 35

1. **a.** 12 **b.** 10 **c.** 3; 15
   d. 2; 14 **e.** 3; 10; 30 **f.** 1; 5; 5
2. **a.** 28 hats **b.** 18 fish **c.** 42 boys **d.** 32 nails
3. **a.** yes **b.** yes **c.** yes
   d. yes **e.** yes **f.** yes

4. 3; 6; 18
5. 15 cups
6. yes

Page 36

1. **a.** 12 **b.** 28 **c.** 36
   d. 2 **e.** 1; 4 **f.** 10; 40
2. **a.** 8 **b.** 20 **c.** 14
   d. 5 **e.** 8 **f.** 6
3. **a.** 20 **b.** 14 **c.** 20 **d.** 32
4. 12
5. 9
6. 6

Page 37

1. **a.** 6 **b.** 0 **c.** 9
   d. 0 **e.** 20 **f.** 16
2. **a.** 28; 32; 36; 40 **b.** 2; 4; 6; 8
   c. 0; 0; 0; 0 **d.** 1; 2; 3; 4
   e. 10; 12; 14; 16 **f.** 12; 16; 20; 24
3. **a.** 2 **b.** 0 **c.** 12
   d. 20 **e.** 16 **f.** 10
4. 0
5. 7; 8; 9; 10
6. 6

Page 38

1. **a.** 60 **b.** 90 **c.** 40
2. **a.** 40 **b.** 25 **c.** 10
   d. 7 **e.** 10 **f.** 9
3. **a.** 5; 10; 15; 20 **b.** 10; 20; 30; 40
   c. 50; 60; 70; 80; 90 **d.** 25; 30; 35; 40; 45
4. 50
5. 12
6. 50; 55; 60; 65; 70

Page 39

1. **a.** 3 × 3 = 9 **b.** 4 × 6 = 24 or 6 × 4 = 24
   c. 6 × 6 = 36 **d.** 12 × 3 = 36 or 3 × 12 = 36
2. **a.** 6 **b.** 60; 6 **c.** 5; 30
   d. 9; 9 **e.** 48; 6 **f.** 18; 6
3. **a.** 30 **b.** 6 **c.** 54
   d. 3 **e.** 7 **f.** 27
4. 5 × 6 = 30 or 6 × 5 = 30
5. 6; 18
6. 6

Page 40

1. **a.** 27 **b.** 72 **c.** 18 **d.** 90
2. **a.–f.** Check expressions for accuracy.
3. **a.** 3 **b.** 9; 6 **c.** 90; 10
   d. 1; 3 **e.** 54; 6 **f.** 7; 7

Answer Key (cont.)

Page 40 (cont.)

4. 45

5. Check expression for accuracy.

6. 3; 9

Page 41

1. a. 21 **b.** 54 **c.** 45

　　d. 18 **e.** 24 **f.** 18

2. a. 12 **b.** 48 **c.** 72 **d.** 30

3. a. 6; 6 **b.** 6; 4 **c.** 8; 4 **d.** 3; 9

4. 12

5. 54

6. 9; 6

Page 42

1. a. 48 **b.** 0 **c.** 32 **d.** 16

2. a. 8 **b.** 4 **c.** 7 **d.** 8

3. a. 16 **b.** 64 **c.** 40

　　d. 80 **e.** 32 **f.** 72

4. 56

5. 10

6. 24

Page 43

1. a. 14 **b.** 28 **c.** 24

　　d. 12 **e.** 20 **f.** 48

2. a. 6 **b.** 32 **c.** 56 **d.** 18

3. a. 8 **b.** 24; 3 **c.** 8; 4

　　d. 2; 5 **e.** 2; 12 **f.** 4; 24

4. a. 20 **b.** 10

5. 36

6. 4; 8

Page 44

1. a. 21 **b.** 35 **c.** 42 **d.** 28

2. a. 0 **b.** 42 **c.** 28 **d.** 70

3. a. 21 **b.** 28 **c.** 56 **d.** 14

4. 49

5. 63

6. 49

Page 45

1. a. 24 **b.** 8 **c.** 25 **d.** 24

2. a. 5 **b.** 30 **c.** 20 **d.** 42

3. a.　　　　**b.**

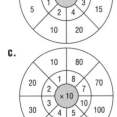

c.　　　　**d.**

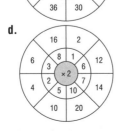

4. 80

5. 24

6.

Page 46

1. a. 1 **b.** 4 **c.** 9

　　d. 16 **e.** 25 **f.** 36

2. a.　　　　**b.**　　　　**c.**

　　area = __4__ squares　area = __25__ squares　area = __9__ squares

3. a. yes **b.** yes **c.** no

　　d. yes **e.** no **f.** yes

4. 49

5.

　　area = __16__ squares

6. no

Page 47

1.

1	②	3	④	5	⑥	7	⊗	9	⑩
11	⑫	13	⑭	15	⑯	17	⑱	19	⑳
21	㉒	23	㉔	25	㉖	27	㉘	29	㉚
31	㉜	33	㉞	35	㊱	37	㊳	39	㊵
41	㊷	43	㊹	45	㊻	47	㊽	49	㊿

d. yes; They are related because 2 × 4 = 8.

e. not a multiple of 8

2. a. 2, 4, 6, 8, 10, 12, 14, 16, 18, 20

　　b. 3, 6, 9, 12, 15, 18, 21, 24, 27, 30

　　c. 9, 18, 27, 36, 45, 54, 63, 72, 81, 90

　　d. 5, 10, 15, 20, 25, 30, 35, 40, 45, 50

　　e. 6, 12, 18, 24, 30, 36, 42, 48, 54, 60

　　f. 7, 14, 21, 28, 35, 42, 49, 56, 63, 70

3. a. 5; 10; 25; 30; 50 **b.** 24; 9; 12; 3

　　c. 40; 20; 32; 36 **d.** 35; 70; 49;

4. 30 is not a multiple of 4.

5. 10, 20, 30, 40, 50, 60, 70, 80, 90, 100

6. shade: 48; 80; 56; 24; 32; 16

Page 48

1. 1 × 12 = 12; 12 × 1 = 12; 2 × 6 = 12; 6 × 2 = 12; 3 × 4 = 12;
　　4 × 3 = 12

2.　　　**3.**　　　**4.**

Page 48 *(cont.)*

5.

All multiples of 4 are also multiples of 2.

6. $48

7. 9; 6

8. 0, 1, 4, 9, 16, 25, 36, 49, 64, 81, 100

9. 1, 2, 3, 4, 6, 12

10. 1, 2, 3, 6, 9, 18

Page 49 possible answers

1. a. **b.** **c.** **d.** **e.** **f.**

2. a. 7 **b.** 2 **c.** 2 **d.** 4

3. a. 2 pieces **b.** 5 pieces

c. 3 pieces; 1 piece **d.** 2 pieces; 2 pieces

4.

5. 5

6. 2 cups; 1 cup

Page 50

1. a. 4 **b.** 3 **c.** 2 **d.** 8

2. a. 6 **b.** 3 **c.** 1 **d.** 12

3. a. 2 **b.** 5 **c.** 5 **d.** 12

4. 4

5. 5

6. 4

Page 51

1. a. 2 **b.** 2 **c.** 5 **d.** 3

2. a.–f. Check drawings for accuracy.

3. a. 5 **b.** 7 **c.** 10 **d.** 6

4. 2

5. Check drawing for accuracy.

6. 7

Page 52

1. a. 3 groups; 1 circle left over **b.** 5 groups; 1 square left over

2. a. 3 **b.** 6

c. 3 remainder 3 **d.** 2 remainder 4

3. a. 3 **b.** 10, 10, 7 (or 9 in each pond) **c.** 2 remainder 7

d. 6 **e.** 5, 5, 5, 5, 5, 2 **f.** 5 remainder 2

4. 2 groups; 1 star left over

5. 2 remainder 2

6. 3 boxes; Check drawing for accuracy: **box 1**–6 ants; **box 2**–6 ants; **box 3**–2 ants

Page 53

1. a. 5 **b.** 7 **c.** 6

d. 8 **e.** 9 **f.** 8

2. a. 4 **b.** 8 **c.** 5

d. 2 r1 **e.** 2 r4 **f.** 2 r4

3. a. 6 **b.** 4 **c.** 8

d. 3 r2 **e.** 3 r1 **f.** 4 r2

4. 9

5. 3

6. 3 r2

Page 54

1. a. 6 **b.** 5 **c.** 2 **d.** 5

2. a. 5; 3 **b.** 6; 4 **c.** 10; 9 **d.** 8; 7

3. a. 4; 4 **b.** 9; 5 **c.** 3; 6 **d.** 10; 10

4. 3

5. 5; 7

6. 7; 9

Page 55

1. Check quotients for accuracy.

2. 4; 2

3. 8 stamps

4. Check drawing for accuracy.

5. Row B is the winning row. The following should be crossed off:

a. 10 **b.** 16 **c.** 6 **d.** 4

e. 42 **f.** 3 **g.** 32 **h.** 2

6. Check quotients for accuracy.

7. Check facts for accuracy.

8.

Page 56

1. a. 51 **b.** 59 **c.** 53

2. a. 37 **b.** 22 **c.** 28

3. a. 15 **b.** 24 **c.** 28

4. a. 4 **b.** 2 **c.** 3

5. 93

6. 78

7. 24

8. 7

Page 57

1. **a.** 14 − 8=6 or 14 − 6=8 **b.** 24 − 9=15 or 24 − 15 = 9
   c. 31 − 24 = 7 or 31 − 7 = 24 **d.** 25 − 17 = 8 or 25 − 8 = 17

2. **a.** 8 + 6 = 14 **b.** 13 + 8 = 21
   c. 6 + 19 = 25 **d.** 19 + 17 = 36

3. **a.** 35 ÷ 7 = 5 or 35 ÷ 5 = 7 **b.** 27 ÷ 9 = 3 or 27 ÷ 3 = 9
   c. 36 ÷ 4 = 9 or 36 ÷ 9 = 4 **d.** 48 ÷ 8 = 6 or 48 ÷ 6 = 8

4. **a.** 4 × 4 = 16 **b.** 3 × 7 = 21 **c.** 3 × 6 = 18 **d.** 5 × 4 = 20

5. 46 − 17 = 29

6. 8 + 16 = 24

7. 56 ÷ 8 = 7 or 56 ÷ 7 = 8

8. 3 × 9 = 27

Page 58

1. **a.** 10; 10 **b.** 22: 22 **c.** 15; 15 **d.** 13; 13

2. **a.** 18; 18 **b.** 8; 8 **c.** 42; 42 **d.** 40; 40

3. **a.** 6 + 4 + 7 = 17 **b.** 18 + 2 + 4 = 24
   c. 17 + 3 + 6 = 26 **d.** 7 + 3 + 8 = 18

4. 21; 21

5. 48; 48

6. 14 + 6 + 9 = 29

Page 59

1. C   2. B   3. C

4. A   5. A

Page 60

1. **a.** 6 **b.** 15 **c.** 34 **d.** 8

2. **a.** 4 **b.** 5 **c.** 4 **d.** 3

3. **a.** + **b.** x **c.** − **d.** +

4. 22

5. **a.** 7 **b.** 10

6. ÷

Page 61

1. 23

2. −

3. +

4. 27 ÷ 3 = 9 or 27 ÷ 9 = 3

5. **a.** 54; 54
   b. 6; 54
   c. 9; 9; 9

6.   **C** is the winning card.

7. **a.** 31 − 5 = 26 or 31 − 26 = 5
   b. 43 − 8 = 35 or 43 − 35 = 8

8. **a.** 9 + 28 = 37
   b. 17 + 6 = 23

9. **a.** 18 ÷ 2 = 9 or 18 ÷ 9 = 2
   b. 30 ÷ 3 = 10 or 30 ÷ 10 = 3

10. **a.** 7 × 6 = 42
    b. 10 × 5 = 50

Page 62

1. **a.** 30, 35, 40 **b.** 90, 80, 70
   c. 8, 16, 32 **d.** 28, 36, 44

2. **a.** add 2
   b. subtract 3
   c. add 10
   d. add 6

3. **a.** add a row of 2 dots on top   **b.** add a column of 3 dots
   c. multiply by 2 **d.** add 1 dot

4. 17, 23, 29

5. multiply by 10

6. **a.** Add a row on the bottom that has 1 more than the row before.

Page 63

1. **a.** 54 − 4 **b.** 35 − 5 **c.** 230 + 6 **d.** 180 + 7

2. **a.** 86 − 80 **b.** 49 − 40 **c.** 508 + 50 **d.** 106 + 80

3. **a.** 427 − 400 **b.** 960 − 900 *or* 960 ÷ 16
   c. 20 + 100 *or* 20 × 6 **d.** 73 + 400

4. **a.** 1,426 − 1,000
   b. 2,385 − 2,000
   c. 160 + 5,000
   d. 291 + 3,000

5. 419 − 9

6. 906 + 40

7. 73 + 500

8. 491 + 6000

Page 64

1. **a.** 717 **b.** 1,455 **c.** 90 **d.** 375

2. **a.** 1,207 **b.** 128 **c.** 327 **d.** 2,263

3. **a.** 324 + 479 = 803 **b.** 441 − 279 = 162
   c. 1,424 − 956 = 468 **d.** 275 + 349 = 624

4. 4,388

5. 3,554

6. 2,477

7. 945 − 489 = 456

Page 65

1. **a.** 297 **b.** 144 **c.** 440
   d. 102 **e.** 34 **f.** 99

2. **a.** 728 **b.** 312 **c.** 126
   d. 42 **e.** 19 **f.** 17

3. **a.** 12 × 15 = 180 **b.** 25 × 35 = 875
   c. 198 ÷ 6 = 33 **d.** 136 ÷ 4 = 34

Page 65 *(cont.)*

4. **a.** 2,884   **b.** 39

5. 106

6. $9 \times 25 = 225$

Page 66

1. **a.** 2   **b.** 1

 c. 6 out of 8   **d.** 3 out of 5

2. **a.** $\frac{2}{5}$ **b.** $\frac{7}{8}$ **c.** $\frac{4}{6}$

 d. $\frac{3}{10}$ **e.** $\frac{1}{3}$ **f.** $\frac{3}{4}$

3. **a.** one half   **b.** four fifths

 c. three eighths   **d.** two thirds

4. 5 out of 8

5. $\frac{2}{6}$

6. one sixth

Page 67

1. **a.** $\frac{1}{4}$ **b.** $\frac{3}{8}$ **c.** $\frac{2}{3}$ **d.** $\frac{4}{8}$

2. **a.**   **b.**   **c.**   **d.**

3. **a.** $\frac{1}{2}$ **b.** $\frac{1}{1}$ or 1   **c.** $\frac{1}{4}$ **d.** $\frac{1}{3}$

4. $\frac{1}{4}$

5.

6. $\frac{1}{1}$ or 1

Page 68

1. **a.** $\frac{2}{4}$ **b.** $\frac{5}{6}$ **c.** $\frac{2}{3}$ **d.** $\frac{4}{8}$

2. **a.** $\frac{1}{4}, \frac{2}{4}, \frac{3}{4}, \frac{4}{4}$ **b.** $\frac{1}{5}, \frac{2}{5}, \frac{3}{5}, \frac{4}{5}$

 c. $\frac{2}{6}, \frac{3}{6}, \frac{4}{6}, \frac{6}{6}$ **d.** $\frac{3}{10}, \frac{5}{10}, \frac{7}{10}, \frac{9}{10}$

3. **a.** $\frac{2}{10}$ **b.** $\frac{1}{4}$ **c.** $\frac{2}{5}$ **d.** $\frac{1}{3}$

4. $\frac{2}{3}$

5. $\frac{1}{5}, \frac{3}{5}, \frac{4}{5}, \frac{5}{5}$

6. $\frac{1}{4}$

Page 69

1. **a.** 3 apples   **b.** 2 strawberries

 c. 3 bananas   **d.** 1 cherry

2. Check that drawings show the following:

 a. 4 tennis balls   **b.** 3 basketballs

 c. 2 golf balls   **d.** 2 baseballs

3. **a.** 4 triangles   **b.** 5 squares

 c. 2 circles   **d.** 1 trapezoid

4. 3 cookies

5. Check that drawing shows 7 balls.

6. 4 diamonds

Page 70

1. **a.** $\frac{2}{4}$ **b.** $\frac{5}{10}$ **c.** $\frac{3}{6}$

 d. $\frac{3}{12}$ **e.** $\frac{4}{16}$ **f.** $\frac{2}{8}$

2. **a.** $\frac{1}{4}$ **b.** $\frac{5}{10}$ **c.** $\frac{2}{10}$ **d.** $\frac{6}{8}$

3. **a.** false   **b.** true   **c.** true   **d.** true

4. $\frac{1}{2} = \frac{4}{8}$

5. **a.** $\frac{2}{8}$ **b.** $\frac{1}{5}$ **c.** $\frac{4}{6}$

6. false

Page 71

1. Check picture for accuracy.

2. yes

3. Check drawing for accuracy.

4. Check drawings for accuracy. Circle $\frac{6}{8}$.

5. $\frac{1}{8}$

6. 2 points

7. 15 cookies

8. false

9. Circle $\frac{2}{8}$ and $\frac{1}{4}$.

10. Circle $\frac{2}{3}, \frac{4}{6}$, and $\frac{6}{9}$.

Page 72

1. **a.** $\frac{6}{100}$ **b.** $\frac{31}{100}$ **c.** $\frac{77}{100}$

2. **a.** shade 12 boxes   **b.** shade 36 boxes

 c. shade 23 boxes   **d.** shade 57 boxes

3. **a.** $\frac{17}{100}$ **b.** $\frac{39}{100}$ **c.** $\frac{97}{100}$ **d.** $\frac{60}{100}$

4. $\frac{70}{100}$

5. shade 47 boxes

6. $\frac{91}{100}$

Page 73

1. **a.** 0.5   **b.** 0.9   **c.** 0.7   **d.** 0.3

2. **a.** 0.1   **b.** 0.4   **c.** 0.3   **d.** 0.6

3. **a.** $\frac{6}{10}$ **b.** $\frac{3}{10}$ **c.** $1\frac{5}{10}$ **d.** $1\frac{2}{10}$

4. 0.4

5. 1.7

6. $\frac{7}{10}$

Page 74

1. **a.** 0.6   **b.** 0.7   **c.** 0.9   **d.** 1

2. **a.** 0.8   **b.** 0.7   **c.** 0.5   **d.** 0.1

3. **a.** 1.1   **b.** 1.8   **c.** 1.6   **d.** 1.5

4. 0.9

5. 0.2

6. 0.3

Answer Key (cont.)

Page 75
1. a. 0.02   b. 0.41   c. 0.96   d. 0.24
2. a. 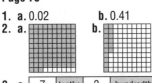   b.   c.   d.

3. a. | 7 | tenths | 3 | hundredths | b. | 1 | tenths | 1 | hundredths |
   c. | 8 | tenths | 6 | hundredths | d. | 4 | tenths | 3 | hundredths |

4. 0.28
5.

6. | 8 | tenths | 4 | hundredths |

Page 76
1. a. 0.4   b. 0.06   c. 0.37   d. 0.61
2. a. 1.1   b. 2.07   c. 2.71   d. 1.33
3. a. 0.2   b. 0.5   c. 0.02   d. 0.59
4. 0.85
5. 1.03
6. 0.51

Page 77
1. a. $\frac{6}{10}$ b. $\frac{9}{10}$ c. $\frac{81}{100}$ d. $\frac{14}{100}$
2. a. 0.3   b. 0.4   c. 0.23   d. 0.74
3. a. 0.2, 0.3, 0.4   b. 0.61, 0.81, 0.90
   c. 1.2, 1.6, 1.7   d. 1.5, 1.9, 2.2
4. $\frac{58}{100}$
5. 0.89
6. 1.6, 1.9, 2.7

Page 78
1. a. true   b. false   c. false   d. true
2. a. <   b. >   c. >   d. <
3. a. <   b. >   c. <   d. <
4. false
5. >
6. >

Page 79
1. a. 0.5   b. 0.8   c. 0.3   d. 0.8
2. a. 1.9   b. 4.7   c. 3.8   d. 3.75
3. a. 3.67   b. 3.97   c. 9.49   d. 3.99
4. 0.8
5. 4.69
6. 3.79

Page 80
1. a. 0.4   b. 0.2   c. 0.1   d. 0.3
2. a. 1.3   b. 1.7   c. 6.2   d. 8.13
3. a. 1.35   b. 1.13   c. 3.12   d. 11.21
4. 0.1
5. 3.61

6. 6.43

Page 81
1. a. 7.5   b. 8.1   c. 7.4   d. 8.84
2. a. 2.8   b. 2.9   c. 5.4   d. 5.18
3. a. 3.9 yards   b. 0.26 yards   c. 4.04 gallons   d. $1.46
4. 8.36
5. 5.18
6. 0.54 gallons

Page 82
1. 0.03, 0.14, 0.32, 0.40
2. $\frac{2}{10}$ = 0.2 $\frac{4}{10}$ = 0.4 $\frac{4}{100}$ = 0.04 $\frac{1}{10}$ = 0.1
3. 0.83
4. 0.2, 3/10, 0.5, 0.7, 9/10
5. circle 1.9; box in 0.11
6. 0.11, 0.19, 0.5, 1.9
7. >
8. $4.15
9. $3.05
10. 0.54

Page 83
1. a. B   b. E   c. A   d. D
2. a. 10%   b. 25%   c. 12%   d. 95%
3. a. <   b. >   c. >   d. >
4. A
5. 45%
6. >

Page 84
1. a. 4   b. 8   c. 40   d. 20
2. a. $1, 25¢, 10¢, 10¢   b. $1, 25¢
   c. $1, 50¢, 25¢, 10¢, 10¢   d. $1, $1, 25¢
3. a.–d. Check that all combinations of coins total $2.25.
4. 4
5. $1, $1, 50¢, 25¢, 5¢
6. a.–b. Check that both combinations of coins total $2.95.

Page 85
1. a. 20   b. 5   c. 10   d. 100
2. a. $50, $20, $5   b. $50, $20, $20, $2, $1
   c. $100, $5, $2, $1   d. $100, $50, $10, $5, $2, $2
3. a. $95   b. $16   c. $51
4. 8
5. $100, $20, $20, $5, $1
6. $121

Page 86
1. a. $3.80   b. $5.35   c. $4.41   d. $3.15
2. a. $4.15   b. $4.15   c. $3.15   d. $4.50
3. a. $2.00   b. $0.40   c. $1.70   d. $2.40
4. $2.53

Page 86 *(cont.)*
5. $5.25
6. $1.35

Page 87
1. **a.** $10.00   **b.** 15¢   **c.** $2.00   **d.** 30¢
2. **a.** 60¢   **b.** $2.00   **c.** 50¢   **d.** $6.00
3. **a.** 5   **b.** 10   **c.** 2   **d.** 1
4. $15
5. $9.00
6. 5

Page 88
1. **a.** $6.00   **b.** $6.00   **c.** $10.00
   d. $3.00   **e.** $11.00   **f.** $19.00
2. **a.** 90¢   **b.** 60¢   **c.** 30¢
   d. 40¢   **e.** 90¢   **f.** 60¢
3. **a.** $4.00   **b.** $ 7.00   **c.** $12.00   **d.** $ 9.00
              + 5.00   + 8.00   + 7.00
              $12.00 $20.00 $16.00
4. $9.00
5. 80¢
6. $14.00

Page 89
1. **a.** $6.00   **b.** 4; $24.00
   c. $6.00; $30.00   **d.** $3.00; $27.00
2. **a.** $9.00   **b.** $10.00   **c.** $12.00   **d.** $12.00
3. **a.** $10.00 – $7.98   **b.** $10.00 – $6.05   **c.** $5.00 – $3.95
      ≃ $10 – $8   ≃ $10 – $6   ≃ $5 – $4
      ≃ $2.00   ≃ $4.00   ≃ $1.00

   d. $5.00 – $2.10   **e.** $20.00 – $16.80   **f.** $20.00 – $10.95
      ≃ $5 – $2   ≃ $20 – $17   ≃ $20 – $11
      ≃ $3.00   ≃ $3.00   ≃ $9.00
4. $2.00; $8.00
5. $12.00
6. $6.00; $4.00

Page 90
1. **a.**   **b.**   **c.**
   d.   **e.**   **f.**
2. c
3. **a.**   **b.**   **c.**
4.
5. no
6.

Page 91
1. **a.**   **b.**   **c.**
2. **a.** C, F   **b.** A, B, D, E, J   **c.** A, C, G, H, I, K
   d. H   **e.** K   **f.** G
3. **a.** 4   **b.** 4   **c.** 3
   d. 6   **e.** 4   **f.** 4
4. **a.** square   **b.** triangle   **c.** circle
   d. rhombus   **e.** hexagon   **f.** rectangle
5.
6. C
7. 4

Page 92
1. **a.** sides = 5; angles = 5   **b.** sides = 5; angles = 5
   c. sides = 8; angles = 8
2. **a.** E, H   **b.** F, G
3. **a.** 10 sides   **b.** 24 sides   **c.** 26 sides   **d.** 35 sides
4. sides = 8; angles = 8
5. A, E
6. 58 sides

Page 93
1. **a.** oval   **b.** trapezoid   **c.** hexagon
   d. triangle   **e.** rectangle   **f.** parallelogram
2. **a.** 4   **b.** 4   **c.** 4   **d.** 4
3. b, e
4. parallelogram
5. B, C
6. 24 angles

Page 94
1. **a.** triangle   **b.** square   **c.** rectangle
   d. triangle   **e.** hexagon   **f.** pentagon
2. **a.** 3   **b.** 4   **c.** 4
   d. 3   **e.** 6   **f.** 8
3. a, b, c
4. rectangle
5. 4
6. Check lines for accuracy.

Page 95
1. **a.**   **b.**   **c.**   **d.**
      regular   irregular   irregular   regular
2. **a.** triangle   **b.** square   **c.** pentagon
   d. octagon   **e.** hexagon   **f.** square; rhombus
3. **a.** triangle   **b.** quadrilateral   **c.** pentagon
   d. hexagon   **e.** quadrilateral   **f.** octagon
4. irregular
5. triangle
6. pentagon

Page 96

1. **a.** smaller   **b.** larger   **c.** smaller   **d.** larger
2. **a.** smaller   **b.** larger   **c.** smaller   **d.** larger
3. **a.** 5   **b.** 3   **c.** 2
   d. 1   **e.** 6   **f.** 4
4. larger
5. smaller
6. 2, 3, 1

Page 97

1. **a.–f.** Circle <u>b</u>, <u>d</u>, and <u>f</u>.
   Underline <u>a</u>, <u>c</u>, and <u>e</u>.
2. **a.–f.** Circle <u>a</u> and <u>f</u>.
3. Correct answers include the following:
   a. A, B, F, G, H, I, M, N   **b.** C, E, J, L
   c. D, K   **d.** F, G, H, I   **e.** M, N
4. larger
5. no
6. A and D

Page 98

1. Circle <u>b</u> and <u>d</u>.
2. **a.**   **b.**   **c.**   **d.**
3. **a.**   **b.**   **c.**   **d.**

Note: Some shapes have more than one pair of parallel lines.

4. yes
5.
6. no

Page 99

1. circle: b
2. **a.**   **b.**   **c.**   **d.**
3. **a.**
   b. no perpendicular lines
   c. no perpendicular lines
   d.
4. no
5. no
6.

Page 100

1. **a.** triangle   **b.** rectangle   **c.** rectangle   **d.** hexagon
2. **a.** sphere   **b.** cylinder   **c.** prism
   d. cube   **e.** cone   **f.** pyramid
3. **a.** 6   **b.** 6   **c.** 3   **d.** 6

4. square
5. cylinder
6. 7

Page 101

1. **a.** square, rectangle   **b.** triangle, rectangle
   c. triangle, rectangle   **d.** triangle
2. **a.** B   **b.** D   **c.** A
   d. B   **e.** D   **f.** E
3. **a.** square
   b. circle
   c. rectangle
   d. circle
4. rectangle
5. C

Page 102

1. **a.** triangle, rectangle   **b.** square
   c. pentagon, rectangle   **d.** octagon, rectangle
2. **a.** cube   **b.** sphere   **c.** cylinder   **d.** rectangular prism
3. **a.** 6   **b.** 6   **c.** 6   **d.** 7
4. rectangle, square
5. cylinder
6. 8

Page 103

1. b, d, e
2. **a.** 6   **b.** 5   **c.** 4
   d. 7   **e.** 5   **f.** 4
3. Check shading of all bases.
   a. 4 faces   **b.** 4 faces   **c.** 4 faces   **d.** 5 faces
4. no
5. 5

Page 104

1. **a.** 6   **b.** 5   **c.** 3   **d.** 1
2. Circle **a.** and **c.**
3. **a.** 4   **b.** 8   **c.** 6   **d.** 12
4. 7
5. yes
6. 6

Page 105

1. **a.** reflection   **b.** rotation   **c.** translation
   d. rotation   **e.** reflection   **f.** translation
2. **a.**   **b.**   **c.**   **d.**
3. **a.**   **b.**   **c.**   **d.**
4. reflection

Page 105 *(cont.)*

5.

6.

Page 106

1. a. cupcake　　　　**b.** cookie

2. a. bottom shelf, right side

　　b. top shelf, left side

　　c. bottom shelf, middle position

3. a. doll　　　　**b.** train　　　　**c.** drum

4. a. bottom row, right　　**b.** middle row, second from left

　　c. middle row, far right　　**d.** top row, middle

5. a train

6. middle row, far left

Page 107

1. a. Northern Territory　　**b.** Tasmania

　　c. Western Australia　　**d.** Queensland

2. a. Diary Mountain　　**b.** Pencil Point　　**c.** Calculator Cove

　　d. northwest　　　　**e.** northwest　　　　**f.** southeast

3. a. go east　　**b.** go west　　**c.** go north

　　d. north　　**e.** west　　**f.** south

4. Victoria

5. Ruler Pier

6. east

Page 108

1. a. 5　　　　**b.** 3　　　　**c.** 2

　　d. 2　　　　**e.** 2　　　　**f.** 3　　　　**g.** 1

2.

3.

4. a. Adam　　　　　　　　**b.** Jo

　　c. corner of Book Rd. and House Rd.　　**d.** Tia

5. go south on Bike Ln.

Page 109

1. a. C　　**b.** E　　**c.** C　　**d.** D

2. Answers will vary; check for accuracy.

3. a. △　　**b.** 🌳　　**c.** ●　　**d.** #　　**e.** ♁　　**f.** ☺

4. E

5. Answers will vary; check for accuracy.

6. @

Page 110

1. a. 2:10　　**b.** 5:25　　**c.** 12:05　　**d.** 8:08

2. a. 35; 9:35　　**b.** 55; 7:55　　**c.** 5; 1:05　　**d.** 40; 11:40

3. a. 　　**b.**　　**c.**　　**d.**

4. 6:02

5. 25; 11:25

6.

Page 111

1. a. 7　　**b.** 14　　**c.** 31　　**d.** 30　　**e.** 31　　**f.** 30

2. a. Monday　　**b.** Saturday　　**c.** Thursday　　**d.** Tuesday

3. a. 31　　**b.** Thursday　　**c.** 29th　　**d.** 4

4. 30

5. Wednesday

6. Saturday

Page 112

1. a. 9:30　　**b.** 10:00　　**c.** 10:30

　　d. 30 minutes　　**e.** 18 minutes　　**f.** 15 minutes

2. a. 7:15　　**b.** 5 minutes　　**c.** 30 minutes　　**d.** 30 minutes

3.

4. 15 minutes

5. 10:45

Page 113

1. a. 2　　**b.** 0　　**c.** 5　　**d.** 6　　**e.** 1　　**f.** 4

2. a. 3 in.　**b.** 6 in.　**c.** 1 in.　**d.** 5 in.　**e.** 2 in.　**f.** 4 in.

3. a.–d. Check lines for accuracy.

4. 3 inches

5. 4 inches

6. Check line for accuracy.

Page 114

1. Check estimates for reasonableness.

　　Measurements:

　　a. 2 cm, 2 cm, 2 cm, 2 cm　　**b.** 3 cm, 2 cm, 3 cm, 2 cm

　　c. 2 cm, 2 cm, 2 cm, 2 cm

2. a. ●—————————●

　　b. ●————————————●

　　c. ●——————●

　　d. ●——●

3. a. centimeters　　**b.** centimeters　　**c.** meters

　　d. centimeters　　**e.** centimeters　　**f.** meters

4. Check estimates for reasonableness.

　　Measurements:

　　2 cm, 2 cm, 2 cm, 2 cm

5. ●———————————————●

6. meters

Page 115

1. **a.** 27 in. **b.** 94 in. **c.** 131 in. **d.** 35 in.
2. **a.** 1 ft. 5 in. **b.** 2 ft. 9 in. **c.** 2 ft. 6 in. **d.** 1 ft. 4 in.
3. **a.** scissors **b.** die, tack, game counter
   c. 6 in. **d.** 2 in.
4. 33 in.
5. 5 ft. 5 in.
6. the pen

Page 116

1. **a.** 12 mm **b.** 28 mm **c.** 35 mm **d.** 83 mm
2. **a.** 1 cm 4 mm **b.** 2 cm 6 mm
   c. 3 cm 9 mm **d.** 1 cm 9 mm
3. **a.** ——————————— · · · ·
   b. —————— · · · · ·
   c. ——— · · · · · ·
   d. ————— · · · · ·
4. 23 mm
5. 5 cm 2 mm
6. ——— · · · · · ·

Page 117

1. **a.** 1 m 23 cm **b.** 1 m 69 cm
   c. 3 m 72 cm **d.** 1 m 78 cm
2. **a.** 2.06 m **b.** 3.42 m **c.** 6.72 m **d.** 1.58 m
3. **a.** 2.7 cm **b.** 240 cm **c.** 4.9 cm **d.** 125 cm
4. 1 m 6 cm
5. 3.75 m
6. 119 cm

Page 118

1. **a.** 3 in. **b.** 4 in. **c.** 3 in.
2. **a.** 20 in. **b.** 13 in. **c.** 6 in. **d.** 7 in.
3. **a.–d.** Check drawings for accuracy.
4. 6 in.
5. Check drawing for accuracy.

Page 119

1. **a.** 4 units^2 **b.** 3 units^2 **c.** 4 units^2
   d. 5 units^2 **e.** 6 units^2 **f.** 6 units^2
2. **a.** 3 yd.^{2} **b.** 5 ft.^{2} **c.** 9 in.^{2} **d.** 16 yd.^{2}
3. **a.** yd.^{2} **b.** in.^{2} **c.** yd.^{2} **d.** in.^{2}
4. 6 units^2
5. 20 ft.^{2}
6. yd.^{2}

Page 120

1. **a.** B **b.** A **c.** D **d.** B, C, D
2. circle: bucket, pool, sink
3. **a.** 5 L **b.** 2 L **c.** A **d.** 3 L
4. A
5. yes
6. 2 L

Page 121

1. **a.** 8 pt **b.** 4 pt **c.** 24 pt **d.** 40 pt
2. **a.** 80 pt **b.** 30 pt **c.** 20 pt **d.** 10 pt
3. circle: cereal bowl, medicine dropper, small jam jar
4. 72 pt
5. 57 gallons

Page 122

1. **a.** 7 **b.** 10 **c.** 27 **d.** 8
2. **a.** 3 in.^{3} **b.** 25 ft.^{3} **c.** 13 yd.^{3} **d.** 1 in.^{3}
3. **a.** 6 in.^{3} **b.** 6 in.^{3} **c.** 10 in.^{3} **d.** 10 in.^{3}
4. 16
5. 17 in.^{3}
6. 4 units^3

Page 123

1. **a.** 6 units^3 **b.** 4 units^3 **c.** 8 units^3 **d.** 6 units^3
2. **a.** c **b.** b **c.** a, d **d.** c
3. **a.** 4 units^3 **b.** 6 units^3 **c.** 8 units^3 **d.** 18 units^3
4. 6 cm^3
5. b
6. 10 units^3

Page 124

1. **a.** 6 **b.** 2 **c.** 3 **d.** 12
2. **a.** pink **b.** brown **c.** pink **d.** yes; yes; no
3. **a.** 4 **b.** 3 **c.** 3 **d.** 3
4. 6
5. triangle
6. 2

Page 125

1. **a.** 4 **b.** no **c.** plain white **d.** dots
2. **a.** false **b.** true **c.** true **d.** false
3.

4. yes
5. true
6.

Page 126

1. **a.** 3 **b.** Friday **c.** Thursday **d.** 2
2. **a.** apple **b.** pear **c.** 5 **d.** 2

Page 126 *(cont.)*

3.

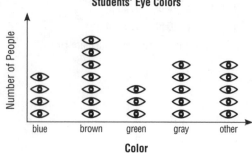

Students' Eye Colors

Key: ◉ = 1 person

4. 9

5. 21

6. brown

Page 127

1. a. brown   **b.** red   **c.** brown   **d.** 19

2. a. 29   **b.** 16   **c.** 45   **d.** 19   **e.** 25   **f.** 27

3.

Insects	Tally	Number
ants	||||| |||||	10
bees	||||| |||	8
flies	||||| ||||	9
butterflies	|||||		6

4. 54

5. 51

6. 33

Page 128

1. a. Chinese and Japanese   **b.** 2

c. 4   **d.** 14

2.

Color	Tally
white	||||| ||||
red	||||| |||
yellow	|||||
green	|||
blue	||||
pink		

3.

Cars in the Parking Lot

←answer for number 5.

4. 24 people

5. Check for 3 additional tally marks in chart and 3 additional cars in bar graph.

6. 7

Page 129

1. a. total number of birds   **b.** 25

c. 49   **d.** addition

e. 25+49   **f.** 74

2. a. total number of plants   **b.** 8

c. 7   **d.** 6

e. multiplication and addition   **f.** 8x7=56; 56+6=62; 62 flowers

3. a. total number of rows of blocks you could make

b. 48

c. 6

d. division

e. 48÷6

f. 8 rows

4. addition

5. multiplication

6. division

Page 130

1. a. 26 big cats   **b.** 71 drinking fountains

c. 35 frogs   **d.** 7 chicks

2. a. 30 cows   **b.** 28 sheep   **c.** 5 chickens   **d.** 6 ducks

3. a. $35.55   **b.** $92   **c.** $37   **d.** $5

4. 93 employees

5. 20 rabbits

6. $1.10